A CIP catalogue record for the paperback version of this title is available from the British Library.  I. S. B. N. 1843862

<u>DREAMTIME</u>

By J. D. Lynch.

<u>CHAPTER 1</u>

My name is John. I was born in a small town called

Hyde, which used to be in Cheshire, but has now been

swallowed up by the Metropolitan Borough of

Tameside, Greater Manchester; a place with two

unfortunate claims to fame: the Moors Murders of the

sixties, and the home of the most notorious serial killer

of all time, Dr Harold Shipman. I was educated at Hyde

County Grammar School in the sixties, and it was here

that an incident occurred that inspired me to write this diary of the events in my life, which provoked the thoughts you may be interested to share with me.

"Can anyone tell me what lies beyond our Solar System?" The question rang out like the retort from a gun. It was being asked by a Physics Teacher of immense proportions, who always smelled of tobacco as he brushed past my desk in the science lab. He was dressed in a shabby pinstripe suite. Why do academics always have to be so, so, different to all the rest of us? This guy was so ordinary that he was different! The school was an old fashioned Grammar School with all the traditional values associated with a sixties educational establishment. "You are one of the privileged few," my Headmaster frequently told me and my classmates. We all thought at the time he was crackers… come to think of it, I still do!

The building was a large, grand, brick fronted mansion style school. I attended there for five years, but never in all that time did I manage to enter through the main front entrance. Only the staff got the privilege of taking that route. All the teachers wore caps and gowns, and whenever one of them entered or left the room, all the pupils stood. You didn't want to antagonise one of them if you could possibly avoid it, believe me. Any talking behind a master's back was usually rewarded with a blackboard duster aimed at your head. They were pretty good shots too those sniper-like teachers.

"Well," he rasped, "Has no-one got an answer?" He looked in my direction and I looked away sheepishly. Too late; he'd already decided I was the one to vent his frustration on. "Lynch, do you have any revelations on what lies beyond our Planets?"

"Space Sir?" I quite proudly answered.

"Well if that's the answer from someone selected to be the cream of our education system, God help the rest. Come on lad, surely you can do better than that."

"We don't know do we Sir, maybe it's just a brick wall." You could tell by now I was getting a little bit more confident.

"You are completely correct in your observation that we don't know, however, if it is a brick wall, what lies beyond it?" he asked. "The human mind is incapable of accepting that infinity can exist. You are programmed into accepting that everything has a beginning and an end. You are born, hence the beginning, you die, hence the end. All things on Earth have a start and a finish. It's not our fault. It's the way the human mind is programmed from birth. If you can open your mind to suggestion, your world will be a completely different place. If I have sown a seed of suggestion in your fertile minds, my job has been a success."

I went home that night not thinking any more of the events of the day. Young men, after all, had other things on their mind, usually associated with the opposite sex. However, on going to bed, I couldn't stop thinking about the question that Mr Whatever his name; asked in that

Physics lab. Now, forty years later, I am still thinking about it.

I woke the next morning and came down the rickety old stairs in our two up and two down, terraced house, to find my mother standing in the kitchen. I could barely see her through the steam filled room. 'Oh no, it was washday, I'm off,' I thought, and with that, I ran back upstairs and jumped back into bed.

I started to think again about the previous day and, before I realised, I had nodded off to sleep again.

CHAPTER 2

I opened my eyes and looked around; it was total darkness. I felt a short sense of bewilderment. I always do when I wake, funny that. My gaze fell upon an old alarm clock sitting on a bedside table. You know the ones I mean, I'm sure you've seen the type. It had two bells on the top, and was probably made in China! I could just make out the fluorescent hands pointing to five minutes past seven. Was it night or morning? It was morning, I remember now; anyway it must be morning I thought, because I could hear someone whistling a tune outside, a Beatles' song if I'm not mistaken. I could hear his footsteps coming up the entry under my bedroom. I say entry because we used to call them ginnells, but I

9

didn't think you would know what I meant if I put that. I heard a thumping noise, and realised it was the coalman; Jim his name was. I looked outside, parting the curtains slightly and saw he was with his two mates, Harold and Cheyenne. We called him Cheyenne after the cowboy series on TV at the time. He wore this massive cowboy hat and leather boots everywhere he went, even in the pub, to which he was a frequent visitor I might add.

As I turned to get dressed, the thumping in my head reminded me of the night before. I had met a few mates and been on what you might describe as a mini pub crawl. A couple of pints of beer in three or four pubs and you can soon inflict a bit of damage on your poor sensory organs the morning after. I was still celebrating the fact that I was now eighteen years and two weeks old, a legal drinker at last. Funny though how it's not as much fun now it's legal. Like most teenagers of the sixties revolution, we had all been having a few swift halves of lager for quite a while before coming of age so to speak. I suppose its part of the ritual of growing up, nice though.

I finally managed to drag a few clothes on and stagger downstairs. Didn't want any breakfast; could I get out before my mum saw me? At the bottom of the stairs, hanging on the banister, was my coat. My pride and joy that coat. It took me eight months to pay for it from my mum's catalogue. As I picked it up, I noticed it was still wet from the night before. It had been teeming down. Still, when you only have one coat and it cost what it did; it has to go on doesn't it? I remember thinking how lucky it was that I had put my coat on last night as I walked home from the bus stop in that torrent.

I wanted to get out early anyway, because I had to go round to my mate's house. The last thing he said to me when he got of the bus last night was, "Don't be late in the morning, be round at my house before eight." We were going shooting that day, just rabbits or anything else we could sell to make a bit of pocket money.

My mate Rick was my best friend. We'd known each other for five or six years and we were more like brothers than friends. He was a tall well built lad, not like me at all. I was a stick insect by comparison, but I did have one thing the same as him; a D A haircut, so called because of the similarity to the rear end of a

duck, if you catch my drift.

 We used to go shooting and rabbitting every week and

we had a kennels on his uncle's allotment. Well, it was a

run-down old shed really, where we kept our precious

lurcher and greyhound dogs and ferrets. That was why

we saw each other every evening. We used to go to his

Gran's house and boil up sheep's heads and any old

scraps of meat we could beg, steal or borrow, mix it

with brown bread or bran and feed it to our hungry

hounds. Anyway, like I said, we had been out the night

before and met a few mates, ending up in a local pub

where we met Rick's girlfriend, Brenda. We all got the

last bus home. He got off two stops before me, to walk

his girl home. I stayed on and then walked home alone in that pouring rain.

'Right,' I said to myself, 'Better not be too late.' He was a stickler for punctuality was Rick.

I walked the ten minutes to his Mother's house. He lived on the same council estate as I did, just a few streets away. I remember when we went to look at our house before we moved from the tiny terraced house where I was born. My Mother refused to accept the fact that there was an inside toilet.

"It's not hygienic," she would say every time anyone mentioned the subject.

"Toilets should be outside where they belong." She would say. Do you know, it was weeks before she used

the loo inside the house, preferring to use the outside
one instead.

All these houses look exactly the same, I thought as I
walked up the steps and around to the back door of his
house. It was a strange thing in those days, how
everyone always used the back door; I guess the front
door was strictly for official business only. I knocked and
waited for a few minutes. The door slowly creaked
open.

"Is Rick in?" I asked rather chirpily.

"You haven't heard have you," came the stuttering
reply. I looked up to see Rick's father standing there,
ashen faced, with tears in his sad swollen eyes. He was

only a small man, but he looked even smaller the way he was hunched over.

"Rick's dead," he sobbed. "He was killed last night. You had better come in lad."

I was shattered; I couldn't take it in initially. I followed him into the lounge where I was met by the sight of Rick's mother and younger brother sitting in two large armchairs, sobbing uncontrollably.

"He was knocked down and killed by a car when he was walking home last night, crossing the road. He was killed instantly. You were with him last night weren't you, John? Tell us what you know will you please."

After about half an hour of telling them about the happenings of last night, and assuring them of the fact that we were not drunk, just a little merry, I couldn't take any more and made my excuses. I had to get out of that house. I walked home in a daze. I don't remember getting home, let alone walking into my mother's house.

As soon as I walked in, my mother saw something was wrong.

"Whatever has happened?" she asked.

"Rick's dead!" I blurted out. The last word hadn't left my lips before I broke down into a blubbering wreck. My mother cradled me in her arms like I was a baby.

"Oh my God" she shouted. That was the first, and to the best of my memory, the only time, that my mother ever put her arms around me. Parents didn't do that sort of thing in those days, did they?

I remember having to go and tell Rick's girlfriend, Brenda, what had happened and how she screamed with horror on hearing of his death. I had to go and give evidence to the cold, seemingly calculated, panel of upright citizens at the inquest; but the most horrific day was the day of the funeral. To see those shabby pink curtains fold around the coffin in the crematorium was the worst thing I had ever experienced in my life. It was the first, but unfortunately not the last funeral I would ever attend. I will never forget that day.

For weeks after, I used to wake in the mornings thinking that Rick was still alive and had only been injured in the accident. I had seen him walking around as clear as daylight. Unfortunately, I soon realized that it was only a dream although it seemed real enough at the time. Sometimes I felt sorry to wake up and return to reality.

I have had many friends and workmates since that time, but none have had the same influence on my life as Rick. Maybe the fact that our friendship was halted so abruptly, and time and familiarity did not have the opportunity to damage it, is the reason for the untarnished bond that still remains between us. Some events in your life are so special and this was one such event. You think of it almost daily, you can't help it. It will be with me forever and had such an important part to play in the remainder of my life. He was my mate!

<u>CHAPTER 3</u>

"Smoko!" came the shout from one of my new workmates. I put down my tools and went for a cup of tea with the other lads I was working with. I must explain that, by this time, I was married with a baby daughter, born to my wife and me when we were both twenty three years old.

One day, in rainy Manchester, I was walking the streets, (I was a postman by the way, not a tramp), when I suddenly had the urge to realise a longing I had had ever since I studied Australia for my G.C.E. exam, all those years ago at school. Well it was only seven years really, but it seemed ages ago at the time. We would emigrate. Could we? Should we? Why not?

 After making enquiries at Australia House, I found out that, at that time, 1972; it was possible to obtain assisted passages Down Under for ten pounds each. After many discussions between my wife and me, and many letters to a friend whom I used to work with, and who now lived in Brisbane, Queensland, he offered to sponsor us and put us up for a while. To cut a long story short, we sold up, and here I was, working on my first day in a truck assembly plant in a place called Wacol, a small suburb of Brisbane.

 I offered a cigarette to the lad who had shouted the initial Smoko announcement a minute earlier.

"No thanks mate, I don't smoke."

"But you shouted smoko a minute ago" I said a little confused. At this point another lad sitting on my left, interrupted.

"You're English?" he asked rather bluntly.

"Yes" I answered.

"Thought so, not been over here long have you?" he said smiling.

"No, a couple of weeks actually. This is my first day at work" I replied.

"Right. Well smoko is the Aussie word for a break time. Are you from Manchester mate?" he asked.

I noticed from his broad Lancashire accent that he must be from my neck of the woods.

"Yes, well Hyde in Greater Manchester actually," I said feeling a bit more confident on hearing a familiar accent.

"Thought so," he answered. That was a phrase used a lot here, I thought.

"I'm from Tyldesley, just down the East Lancs. Road from you," he said.

That was the beginning of a long friendship between Will and me. We used to visit each others houses and have family days out together. He helped me a lot to settle into my new life. Funny though, when I returned to England years later, we lost touch and I don't know where he is now.

Anyway, on those break times, or smokos, I suppose I should call them, our little group used to talk of many things, but the one subject that really fascinated me then, and even to this day, were the things that Bob, the guy who had shouted Smoko on that first day, (and every other day actually), used to tell us about the Australian Aborigines and what a strange, fascinating people they were.

There were two Bobs in our little group: Aussie Bob and Pommie Bob, so named for obvious reasons. Pommie Bob was very quiet and hardly ever spoke, the complete opposite to the effervescent Aussie Bob, we couldn't shut him up. He was a massive guy, jet black hair and a thick black beard; a typical rugged Queenslander, not the type of guy to pick an argument with, if you catch my drift. He had served in the Aussie army in Vietnam and was always telling us of his near death experiences over there, but the less said of those the better. We struck up a quick friendship, Bob and I, because I used to breed Greyhounds with my old mate Rick, all those years ago, and he bred them also. He was fascinated by the fact that I used to go to hare coursing events in England like the Waterloo Cup at Altcar near Liverpool. Hare coursing was illegal in Queensland; in fact you weren't even allowed to keep pet rabbits there.

"You know, of all the states in Australia, I have to live in the one with no rabbits," he once said to me.

"There are thousands of rabbits in Australia, but not a bloody one in Queensland."

"How come?" I asked.

"They built a rabbit and Dingo fence all around the state didn't they? The longest fence in the world that one, just my luck," he groaned. A mine of information was big Bob.

"Right then Bob, tell us about these strange things you know about the Aborigines will you?" I asked him one day on one of our now ritualistic smokos.

"Geez John, they really are a strange lot you know," he bellowed.

"You know, we had a darkie working with us a while ago. He would be fine for weeks, and then all of a sudden he'd vanish for a couple of weeks. No phone call, nothing. When he showed up for work again, the foreman would ask him where he'd been and all he'd say was, 'Sorry boss, I've been walkabout.'

"Another time, he'd been off sick a couple of days. When he came back in, I asked him if he'd been walkabout again."

'No, I had the bones pointed at me,' he said.

'You what, mate?" I asked him.

'I had the bones pointed at me,' he repeated. 'If someone has a grudge against you, they get the witchdoctor guy to point the bones at you. You don't

27

know he's done it, you just get real crook. I've even known some people to lie down and die. The only way you can get rid of the spell is to get someone to find whoever put it on you and pay him to take it off.'

"Sod off," I said to him.

"No, I'm not kidding, it's really heavy stuff," he said.

By this time I could see we had the attention of my Mancunian mate, Will. When he had something to say, which wasn't very often I might add, his shining, baldy head would begin to nod up and down rhythmically.

"It's true is that. I've been in this country long enough to have picked up a few things." Will said in an unusually knowledgeable tone.

"You see the darkies as they call them here; believe in what they call Dreamtime. It was the time when man first inherited the earth. They talk to their ancestors and communicate with people who've died. They have these holy places where they go, to communicate with these dead ancestors, full of cave paintings and bark paintings. They have tribal totems and songs and dances.

"When the English settlers arrived, they took a lot of these places from the Aborigines. Any that objected, were dealt with really cruelly. Have a look at any state map, mate; you'll see places called Ambush creek or Hanging gully and things like that. Sunday morning sport was hunting and shooting, but the prey was human a lot of the time. The blacks over here are still treated badly, you know. I read in a book the other day that one in

every four infant deaths is an Aboriginal child."

"What about you, Bob, do you believe in this

Dreamtime thing?" I asked.

He answered in a more serious tone;

"Well it certainly makes you think doesn't it? Some

people say that, as the western world advanced their

civilisation in a material way, the Aborigines advanced

theirs on a spiritual footing. For thousands of years they

advanced their minds and physic powers instead of

worrying about the more material side of life. Who

knows what's possible? There are certainly many

cultures we don't know much about, aren't there?

We've all heard of black magic but I bet none of us here

could tell the rest what it is. I know one thing though;
these darkies know something we don't."

I have thought frequently about those Aborigines in
Australia over the years. Not much is written about their
way of life. I think they are an embarrassment to the
Australia Government because of the way they were
treated over the years; much the same way the
Americans treated Red Indians.

In the whole of Australia, nowadays, the majority of
Aborigines live on Territories and reserves, usually in
isolated places of no use to the industrialised society.
Some are in Northern Territory, at Arnhem Land,
probably the largest reserve, some in northern Western
Australia and the far north of Queensland. A few work

on cattle stations, and a few have entered the professions and government, but many remain unemployed. I've always been of the opinion they got a really bum deal. Maybe, though, they and other minority groups will have the last laugh come the day of reckoning, so to speak.

Anyway, to carry on, I soon had more important things to worry about other than putting the world to rights.

My wife gave birth to a bouncing baby boy about eleven months after our arrival down under. I put this down to the fact that my mate's house, where we stayed for a few months after our arrival, did not contain a TV set. Maybe, maybe not. It could have been fate, who knows, but this fact, together with us experiencing the worst floods to engulf Brisbane for eighty years, and which scared me to death, made us come to the decision to return to the UK. I have, however, never forgotten my time down under. What a brilliant experience it was; and thanks to Aussie Bob and all my mates, I returned a much wiser, and, I think, a much more thoughtful person than before I went. We were certainly much richer, and I don't mean financially.

# CHAPTER 4

"Stop the car, stop the car now!" She shouted.

The sudden exclamation came from Ann, my long suffering wife, as we were driving into Manchester. It had been about fifteen years since we had returned from our time in Australia, and my son and daughter, Joe and Jean, were now well on the way to becoming normal well adjusted teenagers; about as normal as hormone filled teenagers can be, that is. My daughter was a student at Manchester University, where she was studying economics, what a clever girl she turned out to be. I don't think she got it from me though. I read somewhere that the intelligence gene can only be inherited from the mother. I think there may be some truth in that.

We were on our way to visit her in her student accommodation, a shared house in Burnage, the home of the famous group Oasis, I believe; not the house, the district you understand. I say 'shared house' in the broadest sense. It was more like a squat really; a typical student retreat.

"What do you mean?" I retorted.

"I want to go back," she shouted. "I have to go to see my mother right now."

Past events had already put the thought into my head that Ann saw and knew things that I didn't.

I remembered how when her father had died a few years earlier, we had run upstairs to find him lying on the bed, his eyes still open, a fixed gaze staring towards the open window. He must have died within the hour and, when we looked down, we noticed his arm was outstretched, as was his index finger, pointing through the window towards the sky.

A few days later, after the funeral, she awoke one morning to tell me that she had just said the 'goodbye' to her father which she couldn't do before he died. She went on to tell me how she had this dream of seeing her father in the back seat of a car, waving to her through the rear window. He shouted as he drove away, not to worry, he was happy where he was, and everything would be OK eventually. I suppose most people can relate to experiences like this after losing a loved one. I, myself had the same feeling when I lost my mother years later, but somehow Ann's dreams seemed more convincing than mine. Hers smacked of reality, mine of fantasy.

 Well, rather than facing the wrath of a wronged spouse, I turned the car around and headed to the hospital into which her mother had been admitted a few days earlier. She had been ill with the terrible illness of dementia for a couple of years. It was heartbreaking sometimes to see how such a fun-loving, caring person had deteriorated into someone who couldn't even recognise her own daughter. How cruel nature can often be, I thought. Whilst in care, she had contracted pneumonia, hence her admission to hospital.

When we arrived at the hospital, Ann asked me to wait in the car while she had a few precious moments alone with her mum. After what seemed like an eternity, although it was probably more like half an hour, she returned to the car and calmly got into the passenger seat.

"How's things?" I asked, not really knowing what to say.

"My mum's just died," she calmly replied.

I was surprised she wasn't crying, but I thought it was not the appropriate time to say anything. I knew instinctively that if she wanted to expand on what she had already said, she would do so of her own accord.

"I was holding her hand as she slipped away, and I've never experienced anything like it before," she stuttered.

"As she went, a tingling sensation ran from her hand through mine and right up my arm, just like an electric shock. I'll never doubt there's life after death again. I know for certain now, I will see my mum and dad again. There is nothing more certain to me than that, if nothing else in life."

As I said before, a few years later, I tragically lost my dear mother. I did not experience quite the same feelings as Ann on that sad day, but I do remember, whilst driving home from the hospital after seeing my mother lying so peacefully on that neatly arranged bed, having an overwhelming feeling of love. A kind of feeling that this was not the end. I remember saying to myself out loud, "I will never doubt you again."

 I don't know who I was addressing these words to, maybe God, although I've never really been a very religious person, maybe something else, but of one thing I'm convinced: I was certain then, and still am to this day, that I was not alone in the car that day.

 There was another strange occasion that made me think my wife's psychic powers were in excess of most, and that was when her younger sister, Margaret, died.

 Margaret was only thirty- four years old when she was so cruelly snatched away from the life she loved to live, by that damned scourge of the human race, cancer. We had always been very close to Margaret and her boyfriend, Max; in fact I think she spent more time in our house than she did in her own.

One cold, dark February night, while walking to the car after visiting her in hospital, (the same one where my mother and Ann's mother had died actually), Ann broke down in tears. I put my arm around her trying to comfort her in the only way I knew.

"I've just said goodbye to my sister," she sobbed.

Margaret died a few hours later, on that cold, empty night.

A few days later, Ann told me how she had dreamed of speaking to her sister the night before. Margaret had loved to travel, she lived for her holidays. She had told

Ann not to worry. That she was very happy where she was; she'd seen her mum and dad and she could now go anywhere she wanted, anytime she desired.

I thought momentarily about the talks I used to have all those years ago in Australia about the Dreamtime thing, and I began to wonder. Why does Ann have all these feelings and such realistic dreams and I don't. Will we ever know the answer to all these baffling questions, indeed, is there an answer?

These tragic losses left us both feeling emotionally battered, and our recovery was slow, but, as time slipped by, and with the arrival of our beautiful, baby granddaughter, Maisy, our lives slowly got back on track, and it was my fiftieth birthday before I could say, 'old Codger'.

"Do you want to go out?" my wife asked.

"No, I'd rather stay in and have a quiet night at home. We could get a takeaway if you want?" I answered. "I feel really tired today; it's been a bad day at work."

I went to the local Chinese takeaway and, when I returned, Ann had set out the table with a large red candle as the centrepiece with all the cards surrounding it. Really romantic that, I thought. I asked who she was expecting. She assured me it was all on my behalf. Full of surprises was Ann, but not much of a sense of humour, I thought, as she clipped me around the ear.

I sat down and looked at my plate of multicoloured Chinese vegetables and noodles. A few King prawns were peering at me from under the spring rolls.

"I don't feel too hungry, love," I said, but I ate my fill, about half, and managed a dessert of lychee, also from the takeaway. I remember feeling really tired.

"Think I'll have an early night," I said wearily.

"Do you want some company?" she asked cheekily.

"No thanks love, not tonight. I'm fifty now you know; got to take it easy; anyway more than three times a year is a bit much for me now!"

"Three times, you'll be lucky!" she gasped.

With that, I dragged my weary, fifty –year- old body,

upstairs and, within seconds of my head touching the

welcoming double pillow, I fell into a deep peaceful

sleep.

# CHAPTER 5

Phew, I thought, I don't want another dream like that again. I'd dreamed of being in a sort of tunnel, rather like a railway tunnel, but with no floor or walls. There was this pinprick of light in the distance and I seemed to be floating towards it. I could hear a voice calling my name, "John, John love," it called faintly. It was more than light though. I can't explain what exactly, but when I reached it, I woke up. I'd been watching a programme on the telly a few weeks earlier about near death experiences; I think that's what put the thoughts in my head. My eyes blinked in the darkness of the sombre bedroom. I turned over and noticed Ann wasn't by my side, but that was nothing new. She often got up in the middle of the night to take a shower. Well, she called

five a.m. early morning; I called it the middle of the

night! "Better get up," I thought to myself, "She'll be

shouting me for breakfast anytime now, and I could do

with a shower myself before the toils of the day."

 I dragged myself out of bed and pulled on my well

worn Levis. Ever since I was a lad, I had always had the

habit of dropping whatever I was wearing directly onto

the floor before falling into bed; sheer laziness really, I

suppose. I made my way in the darkness to where I

thought the light switch was, but after groping around

for a few seconds in the pitch black, I couldn't find it.

That's very strange I thought, but after convincing

myself I was still half asleep, I managed to find the door

handle, pressed it slowly and opened the door.

"Where the hell am I?" I shouted.

"Ann, are you there?" No reply.

I can't understand this. I don't remember going out last night, and after living in a bungalow for twenty odd years, you don't expect to be standing at the top of a flight of stairs when you get up in the morning, do you? "These are someone else's stairs," I thought. Talk about stating the obvious... but whose are they?

I made my way apprehensively down the stairs. "Strange this," I thought, "This staircase and landing seem somewhat familiar." At the bottom of the stairs was a long dark hallway. Coats were hanging on the banister, one was soaking wet. A shabby worn carpet had been placed behind the front door to act as a doormat. Under the staircase, hiding in the darkness, were two old gas and electricity meters; the type which you fed regularly with two shilling pieces. I reached out and took hold of the brown plastic doorknob, about twelve inches to my right. As I turned it, rather warily, the door creaked open and I stepped inside.

'I know this room,' I thought. I must be dreaming because as I looked around memories came flooding into my mind.

The room was only small and somewhat cluttered. There was a coal fire burning in the grate of the tile surrounded fireplace. A large domed; mesh fireguard had been placed in front of it to stop any cinders falling onto the rug in front. On the mantelpiece were framed photos of me and my brothers and sisters when we were kids, and in the middle was an old-fashioned green vase. As I looked around, I noticed there was an old, sixties-style radiogram in the corner. The type where you lifted the lid up to use the record player inside. The TV was on. Top of the Pops was playing. It was P.J. Proby singing 'Hold me'.

By this time I knew I was having a dream, because this was my mother and father's house, where I had lived from about twelve years of age until about nineteen when they moved. Not only that, but, what with the soaking wet coat on the banister rail, and the programme on the telly, I realised it was the time my old friend Rick had died. "Thank God for that," I thought, "At least it's a dream and I'm not going crazy just yet." Then I heard a noise which made me turn towards the doorway across the other side of the room. The door handle turned slowly, and the door opened. There, framed in the doorway, stood a tall figure. The light from the flames of the fire flickered across his craggy, somewhat handsome features and lit his Teddy boy haircut which topped his long slender head. "He really looks like my old mate from the sixties," I thought. "No, even more than that, I think it is, yes it definitely is, it's Rick!"

He walked into the room, flicking on the light switch as he brushed past it.

"All right mate," he said, quite nonchalantly, smiling from ear to ear.

"Why am I having this dream? I haven't had a nightmare like this for twenty odd years," I said to myself, but out loud.

"That's not nice calling me a nightmare, is it? I thought I was your mate," he joked. "Don't worry John, this is no dream. You know what's happened don't you? Not to put too fine a point on it mate, you're dead."

"What do you mean dead? No I'm not. I'm dreaming," I bellowed.

"OK then, if you're dreaming, why don't you wake up?" he laughed.

By this time, I must admit, I was feeling a little scared. I could feel my bottom jaw dropping almost to my chest.

I slumped back onto the old, black imitation leather settee.

"I can't take this in," I stuttered.

"Yeah, it is a bit of a choker ain't it? I felt the same when it happened to me," he replied.

I could feel my eyes filling up and I was beginning to feel a knot in my throat.

"What about my wife and kids?" I gasped.

"Don't worry mate, you'll see them again, honest. Just try to relax a bit. Here, have a fag."

He pulled out of his pocket a small green packet of cigs. I remembered that packet. They were Woodbines.

"Bloody hell, I haven't seen those for over twenty years," I exclaimed.

He laughed and handed me a cigarette, passing me a box of Swan Vesta matches in almost the same movement. I lit up a fag and took a deep drag. "That tastes good," I said to myself. It seemed to calm my nerves a little, also.

"If I'm dead, why am I here in my mum's old house? This isn't now, it's … I don't know when. The sixties probably. And why are you here? Why can I see you so clearly? I can't believe I'm having this conversion." By this time, you can probably tell, I was beginning to panic a little again.

"OK mate, calm down and I'll try to explain a few things. When you die, to put it bluntly, your spirit or soul or intelligence or whatever you want to call it, lives on. It doesn't die with your body does it? I know you believe that, because we used to talk about it years ago, right? Obviously, it doesn't have a body or eyes or anything, so what you see or hear doesn't exist in reality. Everything you see or hear or experience will be how you remember it or have imagined it."

"Hang on, I'm not having this, this isn't real!" I shouted.

"Listen mate, the only way I can think of to show you I'm telling the truth, is for you to go to the front door and open it," he said, quite sincerely.

I looked around and noticed the curtains were closed. "Rather than go to the door, I'll open the curtains," I thought, and with that I spun around and threw back the dark green heavy drapes.

What I gazed on was something no-one could have ever dreamed up. The sky was filled with lights of a thousand colours, pulsating and moving in rhythmic vibration. The only thing I've ever seen of any comparison was on a TV programme, I once watched about Jellyfish, of all things. One of them had tentacles pulsating with dozens of shades of fluorescent light; but this sight was something else. This was a million times greater. Imagine all the colours of the spectrum in a rainbow, shining with a brilliant brightness. Add a thousand colours, some of which I've never seen before and can't describe (because there aren't any words in the English language to describe them), and then multiply that by a million fold. Every now and again, all the colours would merge into a brilliant white light and then separate again.

"Good God, what's that?" I gasped.

"That, my mate, is what we call the Perihelion. It's the ultimate point you can go before you start coming back. It's what you know as Heaven."

"But why are we here in my mum's old house, the two of us?" I asked.

"Well I'm no expert, but I think it's maybe because, when you snuffed it, if you'll excuse the term, your thoughts reverted to the things you associated with death. Maybe with us being such good mates, and my accident being your first experience of losing someone close, your first thoughts were of me and your mum's house. I'm here to help you in any way I can, mate. Do you know, you can now go anywhere and see anyone you wish to, anytime you want to? Don't forget though, you won't see or hear the actual person or place or thing. You'll see or hear what you remember it to be, or, what you imagine things to be. After all, you can't see or hear and all that if you're dead, can you?"

My mind momentarily flashed back to the time my wife told me about the dream she had had, in which her sister, Margaret, told her that she could now go anywhere she wanted, whenever she chose.

"All you have to do is think of someone or something for a while, wish you were there, shut your eyes, open your mind and 'hey presto' it'll happen. What I did when it happened to me, was try to think of someone who is dead, obviously, and who can answer your questions about what's happened to you and what lies ahead for you, because, I can tell you now, John, this is not the end. I can help you as much as I can, but I'm sure you'll be able to think of more suitable people to help you other than me. If you remember mate, I never pretended to be the sharpest knife in the drawer, did I? One thing I can promise you though, you'll be happy here once you come to terms with it John. This is where we all end up. This is where we all belong. This is our destiny. This is the Perihelion."

After a little more small talk about events back home since he left, and chatting about old times, Rick said he could see I was tired, and suggested he leave me alone for a while to let me come to terms with events.

He got up and slowly walked towards the door, pausing to look back as he went through.

"Don't worry John, I'll see you again soon," and with that he disappeared. I heard the front door close, and closed my eyes for a moment. I can tell you, it was a very troubled few hours I had after that. Next, before I knew it, through sheer exhaustion I fell asleep, so tired and confused. "What will happen next?" I thought as I nodded off, "What's this all about?"

CHAPTER 6

I woke, after what seemed to be only a few minutes, to the sound of the sea washing against the rocks. As I looked around, I saw I was sat by a large tree. There were rocky outcrops along the shoreline and I noticed a number of large, lizard- type creatures, seemingly sunbathing on these rocks and, occasionally grunting hoarsely to each other. They didn't seem to have any fear of me; in fact I think I was more afraid of them. I wondered if they could see me as clearly as I could see them. A small bird was flitting around the tree I was sitting by; it had a small twig in its little beak and seemed to be using it as a tool to poke into cracks in the

tree's bark.

"Where am I now?" I said to myself.

"You're in the Galapagos Islands," came the surprising

reply.

The sudden outburst took me by surprise. I hadn't seen

anyone around. I turned to see a rather large old man

sat on a log behind the tree. He looked to be about fifty

or sixty years old, but he was one of those people that

it's hard to put an age to. You know what I mean; a

typical Victorian type of chap. They all look the same

age, don't they? He sported a large, bushy, grey beard

with eyebrows to match. The same colour as, what was

left, of his thinning mantle. He was dressed in a dark

grey, double breasted suit, with a white, starched shirt,
shining from beneath in the bright sunlight. Somehow
he looked a little foreboding.

"I recognise you; you're Charles Darwin, aren't you?" I
said, rather pleased with myself at this bit of astute
recognition."

"You know who I am then? You should because it was
you who wanted to speak to me, wasn't it?"

"Yes, I recognise you from a picture I saw in a textbook
at school" I answered.

"I see you remembered the lizards and birds that use
tools, which helped me form my theories on evolution
as well," he chuckled, nodding to the rocks nearby.

"How right you are, and yes, I would appreciate your help if you would be so kind." I said.

"You know you only see what you remember or imagine here, don't you? That's why you see me as the person you remember in that book, but that doesn't matter, how can I be of help to you, my little friend?"

I thought he sounded a little condescending, but when you're as famous a person as he is, I suppose you have the right to be, don't you?

I explained that I had only just arrived, but I think he knew that anyway from my stupid -sounding statements to date, and I told him that I was having trouble coming to terms with what had happened over the last few hours. Was it hours or was it days, who knows?

"I understand. We've all been through it at some time you know" he said rather thoughtfully.

"Let's start from the beginning, and take it from there, one stage at a time, shall we?

"You see, John, all the universe, every star, every planet and all life forms down to the smallest atom, is made up of pure energy. Indeed all the planets and stars were formed when two kinds of energy collided, multiplying millions of times with a force unimaginable, and then slowly cooling and solidifying over millions of years. Our own human race is made from pure energy; our minds are also made of the same pure energy. Energy cannot be destroyed, only changed to another form. The human mind, all our thoughts, are not physical, and are so near the pure form of energy that they remain exactly the same after we die.

"I think everyone now believes that life on earth started in the oceans, don't you agree? If you've read any of my books, or heard of my teachings, you'll know that I believed in the theory of natural selection and survival of the fittest. Well, I was pleasantly surprised to see how close to the truth I was when I wrote those things, now that I can see more of the whole picture, so to speak."

"But if, as you say, we, the human race, are descended from apes and monkeys, how come we appear to be the only creatures to question where we come from? The only ones with intelligence?" I queried.

"We're not. How do you know we are?" he answered, rather abruptly.

"Think about plants on Earth. They have no eyes, but they grow towards the light and know which way is up and down.

"You don't know what other animals are thinking do you? And there are many other galaxies, besides ours, in the universe, many of which are much older than our Milky Way. You do know, don't you, that scientists on earth have now proven that there are more stars in the universe than there are grains of sand on earth? Well, I can tell you, you can multiply that by forever.

"You see John, yes, I know your name by the way; all life is born with the will to survive. The goal for all life forms is to achieve everlasting life here, in the Perihelion, or heaven as you may know it. All forms of life have to evolve in their own way to achieve that goal of the ultimate existence. There is no option; it's programmed into the DNA of all life. It's the essence of all life; it's the destiny of us all.

"The whole basis of evolution is that, every now and then, a freak of nature in a species is born. This freak is, however, accidentally sometimes better equipped to survive than others of its kind. So therefore are its offspring. Therefore these freaks of nature gradually replace their ancestors, and so the change goes on."

"What do you mean by the ultimate existence?" I asked.

"Imagine if you can, for example, you could chop off someone's head and keep it alive artificially. The brain with all its thoughts and memories would still be alive, wouldn't it?" he answered.  "Then go one step further and take out the brain and keep that alive. The thoughts and intelligence would still be there again, wouldn't they? You couldn't see or hear or touch, but you would still remember what all your senses were and felt like wouldn't you? Imagine then, that we could go the final step and keep that intelligence alive without the brain. Hey presto, here we are, the ultimate existence. No physical body to hold us back, no struggle for life to hinder us, no need for laws to fight crime, no jealously or hatred, just living in perfect harmony.

"Some say the best way to start on the journey of achievement must be to adapt to reproduction without sex, a single sex society. Some species have begun this already. Do you know John, there are a variety of fishes in the sea on Earth, that swim around in massive shoals, and all are females except one, which is male. When he dies, one of the females takes his place and changes sex to become a male. On another occasion, a deep sea fish was discovered, that lived on the bottom of the ocean. Scientists were baffled as to why they could only find females until, one day; someone noticed a tiny lump on one of the fish's sides. It turned out to be the male; there are many species on Earth that have perfected how to reproduce without sex. Indeed humans seem to be on their way to this also, with cloning and other scientific techniques.

"I think the next step after that, will be to achieve everlasting life. Death must become a thing of the past. This is a requisite of man expanding his knowledge, by not dieing before his work is finished. Imagine what could be achieved if someone like Einstein could have carried on his work after his lifespan. The possibilities would be awesome."

"Why then must all forms of life take all this trouble to achieve what you say is the ultimate goal, life everlasting in heaven, if we all come here when we die anyway?" I asked.

"Planets and stars only have a limited life. All stars die eventually, and along with them their planets. The aim for all forms of life is to achieve the ultimate existence before their host planet dies. I know millions of years may seem a long time, but, in terms of the universe, it's just the blink of an eye. Many species from all over the universe have not made it in time. Their stars have died and so have they. Some are here that came before their planet died, but no more will come. Only when a species has attained the required intelligence level to exist in the ultimate form, (that's without a body and life everlasting to you and me), will they be able to see the whole picture. No species from Earth can see it, because no-one, or thing, has yet attained that level; but all life must carry on struggling to get there before they become extinct for one reason or another.

"Compare life to baking a cake. To bake a cake, you must take all the ingredients measured in specific quantities, place them into a container and bake them for a set time in an oven. So also with life. We must take the entire chemical and molecular components in critical quantities, place them in a container, (the body), and process them for a set time in an oven, (the planet Earth). At the end of the process, death, we hopefully have a soul. Many things can happen to interrupt this process and that is the reason we don't get a perfect spirit, but one day, it will happen. We must continue to strive for this. We have to continue to produce intelligences to meet this end because, eventually, there will be an almighty explosion of energy and life. The universe will change irrevocably forever, in a way we cannot imagine. That is the reason for the urgency."

"I know I may sound stupid but I hope you don't mind answering my questions like this sir?" I said rather meekly.

"I don't mind at all. At least you want to know, which says something about you, doesn't it?" he replied.

"Well then, if all these souls, or intelligence's, come here, how do they all fit in?" I asked.

He laughed.

"You must rid your mind of the human thoughts that everything has a beginning and an end. The Universe is endless. There is no such a thing as empty or full. You can't fill up something that goes on forever can you?"

'Bloody hell,' I thought, 'That old physics teacher of mine at school was right after all, wasn't he? I wonder if he's here? Suppose he must be somewhere. I bet he's pretty pleased with himself now.'

"When you mentioned freaks in evolution, what exactly did you mean?" I asked.

"Well John, let's look at the human race for example. Could you have composed a concerto at thirteen years of age? Could you have painted the ceiling of the Cistine Chapel like Michelangelo? Could you have written poetry like Keats or Shelly? Could you have written a song like Bob Dylan or John Lennon, and could you have out boxed Mohammed Ali? Need I go on? All these people were not average human beings were they? They were different, in other words freaks of nature. In some instances, there are, on occasions, people born who surpass even the realms of the genius of those I have just mentioned; however there are persons here far more qualified to tell you about them than I am. I'm sure you'll meet someone to explain this later."

'This man is beginning to make sense,' I thought to myself. I was now becoming a little more optimistic, and felt a little more secure and confident.

"How do you explain people seeing ghosts and UFOs? Are they imagining these things, or are they simply not telling the truth?" I asked.

"No not really. You see, in the human mind, there is more of the brain unused than used. Some people, although not freaks in the way I described earlier, can utilise parts of this latent brain and partly connect with someone here in the Perihelion. They don't understand what it is they see, only that there is some sort of thought they have experienced. Maybe, to them, it's like catching a glimpse of the greater picture. These flashes of connection are interpreted differently by people, according to how their brain has been educated and influenced by the life they have led. Some will see UFOs, some may see ghosts, some will even imagine they can communicate with people who have died, but no-one will be able to consciously connect fully with us here, except in very special cases, about which you may learn later, maybe.

"The nearest most of us get to seeing these things is in our dreams, when parts of our minds are open to accept subconsciously things that they cannot accept in a conscious state."

My mind flashed back to those dreams my wife told me she had had about her Father and Sister. I always knew she could see things I couldn't. If only we knew then what I know now. How it could have saved us all those weeks of worrying and depression. She wasn't ill or going mad, she was special.

I also thought of the Aborigines 'Dreamtime' we used to talk of in Australia. Could it be that their minds are so advanced compared to Europeans that they already have one foot on the first rung of the ladder to eternal life, and if so do they know it?

"You see John, that's why, even after hundreds of years of the finest brains using the most sophisticated technology known to man; no-one has, or ever will, make contact with what you call extra- terrestrial life. They are quite simply looking in the wrong place, with the wrong equipment. Scientists must change from trying to reach other planets physically. It will never happen. Yes they may land a man on Mars or even another planet but to what avail? They must start to concentrate on developing the intellect of man by making life everlasting, so that they can carry on learning forever, and existing without the confines of a physical body. That is the only way forward. The change must be made now, and there is no time to waste. It will probably take thousands maybe millions of years to achieve, and the way the human race is going it may not even have the time until the Earth dies. They will exhaust the resources or pollute it so much that they will become extinct before that happens. I fear sooner rather than later. I, as a scientist, fear for the human race. I am beginning to doubt whether they can change direction in time. I just hope that if they do destroy themselves, they don't destroy the planet along with them so that some other species has a chance to achieve their goal of ultimate existence."

'Well thanks for that bit of optimism,' I thought, 'I hope the next person I meet is not as cheerful. Can't take too much frivolity in one go.' And with that I closed

my eyes and slipped into a sort of trance. I thought, as I

lay there, that all these things certainly made sense, but

one major question remained one that I must seek the

answer to. What about religion? Where does God figure

in all this, I wonder?

CHAPTER 7

I opened my eyes and awoke from my semi-trance. When I say awoke, it wasn't like waking from sleep, it was more like leaving one dream and slipping into another. Anyway, I looked around and found myself standing on this rocky pathway. On both sides of me were sandy banks, a few withered shrubs scattered around the parched grey fields, and an odd olive tree here and there. I could see a group of people in the distance. As I approached, one of them seated on a large rock, appeared to be speaking to the others, and as I got nearer, this man rose and walked towards me.

As he got closer, I could see he was a tall man, slim build, dressed in a long cream coloured robe, one end thrown over his shoulder, the other dragging on the dusty earth track. His features were dark and swarthy looking, somewhat Arabic, with a short black beard and long dark wavy hair. I recognised him immediately from the many pictures I had seen over the years. It was the man I knew as Jesus of Nazareth.

"Hello, you're Jesus aren't you?" I thought immediately what a stupid thing to say, but I couldn't think of anything else.

"Hello, yes I am. You're John aren't you? Welcome," he answered.

"Come; let's take a walk along the path."

"What about your friends?" I asked, looking at the group of people he had just left.

"Oh they will be fine; most have been here for quite a while. I feel you are in need of my help more than they are right now. I sense you are worried. Can I help?" he continued.

"I've only just got here and I'm missing my wife and family terribly. To be honest, I'm really scared I won't see them all again and I love them so much. I felt a little better after speaking to Mr Darwin, but now I've begun to feel really down again." I said rather gloomily.

"John, let me assure you, here and now. I promise you will see all your family again, in the future when they all will join us here. Don't worry how you feel; it's understandable, you've been through a lot in the last few days. We all felt the same at first." he said.

He spoke in a way that seemed to give me a little more confidence, as though he knew what he was talking about.

"Were you the same?" I asked.

"Well yes, but not exactly, but more of that later," he answered.

"Why, because you are the son of God?" I said.

"Let me ask you a simple question, John. What do you understand God to be?" he asked.

"I'm not sure. Being brought up as a Christian, I was taught to believe that God is the Supreme Being, he controls everything, but no-one knows what he looks like, do they?" I answered.

"You keep referring to God as He, as if you believe God is a person. Look around you, all these spirits or souls let's call them, from all over the universe, all existing in perfect harmony. This is God; we are all God, living in what we call the Perihelion, you may know it as heaven. Yes I am the son of God, you are the son of God, we are all the children of God. God is not a being or person, God is all of us, do you understand, John?" he said quite emphatically.

"But you died on the cross and rose again from the dead didn't you, or is all that not true?" I asked.

"John, let me tell you about my life and then, maybe, you'll understand a little more.

"Do you remember Darwin saying something about the special people? Well, every now and again, and I must emphasise, it is a very rare occurrence; someone or something is born, to quote Darwin, as a freak of nature. I don't mean in a physical sense, but in a mental or spiritual sense. They can see much more than normal. They know of all this, here. They have the ability to use all of the normally latent parts of their brain to connect with a spirit here. This is always a relative or ancestor from whom they inherited some of their intelligence genes. The spiritual bond can be phenomenal, even, sometimes, to the extent of the two being as one in life and death. They see this from birth and many try to tell others in their lives about their knowledge of life and death. Unfortunately most are treated as cranks or fools, some are ignored, some are ostracised, some are even persecuted and killed. I was one of those people.

"I was born in Bethlehem, just as it says in the bible. The ancestor with whom I had formed a connection was of royal descent from the east. On hearing of my birth, three relatives came to see the new royal infant. They came and left, in as much secrecy as they could, for the Romans, and others, were fearful of uprisings instigated by the arrival of any leaders from the traditional monarchy. Any discovered were often killed immediately."

"The three Kings from the Orient!" I shouted excitedly.

"Yes, John; we hurriedly moved to Nazareth, where I lived, moving around, preaching my knowledge to anyone who would listen, and gaining a group of followers along the way. Don't forget, John, I lived in a time two thousand years or more before you were born. This was a time when people had no T.V. or newspapers as you had. The only means of communication was by word of mouth. Most could not read or write; many truths got distorted along the way. If you questioned the establishment, that was the church or the governors, you were severely punished. It was a time when women were stoned to death for adultery. Chopping off the hands of thieves and crucifying criminals was regarded as normal. It was thought correct to sacrifice animals to God. That's why I spoke to my followers in parables and stories, in a way they could understand. People were much more naive in those days; they were more open to suggestion, which is why most major religions are thousands of years old. If it happened in your day anyone preaching religion would probably be ignored or branded a crank. From the knowledge I had, and from what I said to my followers, it must have seemed I was not a normal man. Little wonder they thought of me as the son of God.

"Anyway, when the church and the establishment heard of my teachings they said I was being blasphemous, and I was finally arrested and crucified by the Romans.

"Mary Magdalene was my partner in life. She was

always by my side, she was my rock. She was with me all

through the crucifixion. It was a terrible day when I was

raised on the cross. I don't think the soldiers were very

happy to be there, to tell you the truth. Some were very

sad to be doing what they had been ordered to do, but,

I suppose they had to. After many hours, she begged

the soldiers to take me down and, believing me to be

dead, they eventually did so. Mary noticed a flicker of

life still in my body, and, after convincing them that I

was dead, she asked for my body so that she could

dispose of it in a dignified way. They agreed. I think they

just wanted to get away as soon as possible, actually,

and Mary, along with friends, carried me to a place that

was safe.

"After many months she nursed me back to health. When I was fit enough, I went to see some of my followers and told them I had to leave, them fearing I may be discovered. After seeing the scars on my body, they thought I had risen from the dead and could not be convinced otherwise. Eventually Mary and I fled to what is now known as the south of France, where we lived together for the remainder of our lives. I didn't realise at the time how my so called 'resurrection' and my teachings to my followers, were going to have such an impact on the world in times to come."

"Do you regret that?" I asked.

"Not all of it" he answered.

"Some good has come from it hasn't it? I think mankind has some sort of semblance of law and order, and I think religion has helped to establish that, hasn't it? My biggest regret is that some people use religion as an excuse to commit atrocities against fellow humans. Most of these people have been brainwashed from birth by others who fear the truth, to be fanatical, religious martyrs, fully believing that what they do is their God's will. The poor souls believe this, even to the extent of killing themselves as well as others. Surely, no-one should be made to believe that God, whatever they believe that to be, could condone man killing fellow man in his name. These misplaced beliefs in numerous Gods have been the cause of so much unnecessary suffering in the world. My only other regret is that I cannot be reincarnated in some way to tell people about what I know, and carry on my teachings and try to end all these troubles on the Earth."

"So there is no reincarnation then?" I optimistically asked.

"No John, unfortunately not. We've all seen children who have mannerisms and looks of their Mothers or Fathers; and sometimes, we may think this is a loved one returned, but it can't happen. You see, John, just as physical characteristics are inherited through DNA from one generation to another, so are some mental characteristics. It's pretty straightforward really. Every new-born baby has some slight connection to a close relative or ancestor, but there is no reincarnation."

"I have one more question if I may? You say everyone comes here when they die, but what about Heaven and Hell, and how we have always been led to believe anyone who commits crime or is evil, cannot go to heaven?" I asked.

"John, I have never said in all my teachings, that Heaven is not attainable by anyone." he answered.

"Quite the opposite. I have always said that everyone is welcome in the kingdom of God, good and bad, rich and poor, black and white, in fact all living creatures.

"I don't know of anyone who can tell me of any other form of life, except humans, where any kind of crime exists, do you? Think of all the animals on earth for example. Yes, some kill others, but only for survival or food. All animals have a code of conduct by which they live. If for example a lioness and her cub stray into another pride's territory, the cub is killed instantly by the resident pride. The mother would be killed also if she did not flee. The cub's carcass is not eaten, so the lions did not kill for food. Some may say this is evil, killing a baby, but it is done to maintain the survival of the species, the sole reason. All actions of animals are controlled by the inescapable drive for survival of the species, with the ultimate goal being to reach the supreme state of existence here. No animal has a choice about that; it's programmed into all life. No normal human being could commit a crime, only those that so-called 'civilisation' has affected the minds of, in some way. Some are affected by the pressures of the family, some by work, some by drugs, and some even by TV,

books or the media. It's not their fault; no-one commits

crime by choice. The basis of most crime is greed,

jealousy and ignorance. If they were left alone and not

bombarded by all these pressures, and if all people

were equal, it could be so different. These people

should be helped instead of punished. How can the

answer be to lock people away, or even kill them? That

is just fear or revenge. The human race must take a long

hard look at itself with regards to crime and how to deal

with it. Prevention is a million times better than cure

after all.

"All souls or minds or whatever you wish to call them,

come here to the Perihelion, free from any

preconceived ideas and thoughts of anything but peace

and harmony. All are equal, men, women, criminals,

animals and yes, even plants and many things between,

from all over the universe. If everyone was equal on

earth as in heaven, maybe that would be the first step

to peace, don't you think? When I said in one of my

sermons, that it is easier for a camel to pass through the

eye of a needle than for a rich man to enter the

kingdom of God, that is what I meant. The message I

was trying to explain is that when our bodies die, we all

come here equal. There is no gain to be made from

acquiring wealth on earth. What does it matter that you

can be rich on earth for fifty or so years at the expense

of your fellow man, when you will be here in paradise

for eternity with everything perfect?

"So you see, John, don't be sad. You can now meet all your loved ones you haven't seen since they died, you can even meet people you may have wanted to on Earth but never got the chance .You can go anywhere in the universe, anytime you desire," he said.

I thought of the dream my wife had of her sister, Margaret, where she had said exactly the same

"One more thing please?" I asked tentatively.

"Darwin said something about only seeing the full picture when a species had attained the knowledge of the ultimate level of life. What did he mean?"

"I cannot explain that to you, John, because your mind is not advanced enough to absorb it.

"I can only tell you something a Greek philosopher once said, it may help.

"Imagine man is a flea living on a dog's back. You live in a warm protected environment, deep in the fur, safe and secure. One day you climb up a strand of hair. You glimpse the outside world and the daylight, but you can't understand what it is. You've only ever seen your dark, safe world, deep in the fur. You can't imagine the world beyond. What do you do? You're frightened by what you can't understand, so you climb back down the hair to where it's safe and warm.

"One day if and when the human race attains the required level of intelligence, someone special will come along to teach us all the full picture of our existence.

How the universe was formed; why we are here; what lies ahead? I can't tell you these things, but I hope the human race can eventually get there, and we will be complete at last. I hope one day we can jump off the dog's back." I'm sorry; John, but I must leave you now. I feel others need my help. We will meet again soon I'm sure. If you need my help you know what to do; just the same as you did before. Goodbye for now."

With that he turned and walked down the path into the distance. He had helped me a lot in those few hours; I was now feeling much better and was actually looking forward instead of back. "Just think," I said to myself, "I'll be able to meet some of my boyhood heroes; Elvis and John Lennon, to name but two. I'll be able to see my mother again whom I miss so much, and my wife's mum and dad and her sister, Margaret, whom we were

so close to." Yes it was definitely getting much better.

<u>CHAPTER 8</u>

As I left this moment behind, I found myself walking along a tarmac path. Privet bushes lined both sides, blocking out any views one could have had of the surrounding area. I recognised where I was immediately. It was the path leading to my wife's mother and father's house. It was the path where my wife and I shared our first kiss; it was our special path. As I walked towards the opening at the far end, I heard a voice behind me calling my name.

"Hiyah, you made it then," someone shouted.

I turned around and there as clear as day, was my wife's sister, Margaret, following me behind, looking just as she did before her illness all those years ago, tall, slim and the picture of health.

"Bloody hell, you look wonderful. I'm so glad to see you again. After you left us, Ann and I never really got over it, you know. Our lives changed forever that night; we missed you so much," I said.

"Well, you'll be OK now. Come on, let's go around the corner, there's someone who'll want to meet you," she smiled.

As we rounded the hedge, there, leaning on the white slatted garden gate of Ann's mum's house, was an old man waving at us.

"Hello lad, bet this is all a bit of a headache to take in, heh? Come over here and give us a look at you," he shouted.

It was Ann's dad, just as he was in the eighties. It was a funny thing with parents in those days, I thought; mine were the same; I could never remember them being young. I suppose people grew up a lot earlier then, they had to. They were mostly married with kids when they were just out of their teens.

"Come into the house," he said.

As I followed him through the front door, I noticed the garden full of rose trees surrounding the deep green, immaculately trimmed lawn. There, at the side of the front door, climbing up the trellis, was the famous pink rose bush. I say famous because, when my wife- to- be was coming out of the house to go to the church on our wedding day, the wind caught hold of her veil and tossed it into the rose tree. She always said it was an omen not to get into the car. I think she was joking, but I was never sure. I went through the door and into the dimly lit hallway. Typical council house of the period, just like the one I lived in during my teens. I turned through the door on my right and entered the living room. There sat in a chair in the corner, warming her legs on the coal effect gas fire, was Ann's mum.

 "You look wonderful," I said to her. She was a beautiful woman when younger; deep blue eyes and jet black hair. They always said, if you want to see your wife in thirty years time, take a look at her mum. Well I'd be happy there, I thought, when we first got married.

"You look well yourself," she replied.

"It's good to see you again," she continued. "I hope Ann wasn't too upset when I died. I so wish I could tell her I knew she was there, holding my hand, that day in the hospital when I had to leave you all. I wish I could tell her in person that everything will be all right in the end, instead of just in dreams. I don't know if she believes me, you see."

"Don't worry, she's seen you all in her dreams and said her 'goodbyes for now' to you all. I thought dreams meant nothing then, but now I know different. Ann always thought that dreams had a meaning. I wish I'd

paid more attention to her at the time," I said.

"Come on, let's go out," Margaret shouted, bursting

into the room. She always was the life and soul of the

party; I could see she hadn't changed a bit.

"Where are you going?" I exclaimed.

"I'm going to Cyprus, come on, "she answered.

Cyprus was the last holiday we all had together with

Margaret and her boyfriend. She had just finished a

course of chemotherapy for her cancer treatment and

we went away to give her a bit of a boost. She always

said it was her favourite place in the world. Come to

think of it, that was probably true for all of us. It's a

magical place steeped in history. I remember our

visiting the Tombs of the Kings near Paphos whilst on that holiday, and marvelling at the way the labyrinths of tunnels and tombs had been carved out of the solid rock. It must have taken hundreds of years and thousands of men to complete that marvel of engineering, with only the primitive tools they had at the time.

"Can I ask you a question?" I asked rather sheepishly.

"Yea, of course you can, John," she replied.

"When you left us, did you and your dad speak to Ann in her dreams?" I asked.

"Yes we did. It's the only time we were able to speak to anyone on earth whom we were close to and had to leave. I think it's something to do with people's minds opening up when they're asleep and being more

receptive. I don't think it's possible when you're

conscious, but it is in dreams," she answered.

"Thanks, Margaret; I do hope she knows how much I

love her. Maybe I'll be able to tell her one day in one of

her dreams."

"I don't see why not. Anyway, are you coming with me

or not?" she asked.

"I'm sorry, but I can't go now. I've got lots more

people to see. I'll come one day though; maybe when all

the family is together again, heh."

"OK well I'm off then." And with that she ran out of

the door and around the corner.

I chatted a while to her mum and dad, filling them in with the events in the family since they left. They were thrilled to find out they had a new great-grandchild, our Maisy. It seemed to comfort them to know everything was alright at home.

"Well I'm sorry, I'll have to leave you now, but I promise to come and see you again soon," I said, and with that I made my way through the door and into the street. I was surprised to find I wasn't on the same street as before. Then again, I don't know quite why I was surprised, after all, "nothing's impossible here is it?" I thought

## CHAPTER 9

I felt as if I was drifting in space. After being on the

street a few seconds ago, here I was, enveloped in a

cocoon of pulsating light, reflecting all the colours of a

million rainbows. It was beautiful if not a little awe

inspiring. As I drifted, as in a cloud, intoxicated by

satisfaction and delight, I could hear a faint voice calling.

I couldn't make out what it was saying at first, but as I

tried to focus my mind on the sound, it gradually

became louder. "John, John," it echoed, "Yes, I know

who this is," I thought, "it's my wife, it's Ann."

"John, I hope you can hear me. I never got the

chance to say 'goodbye,' did I?  But I can see you now,

as clear as daylight. Have you really gone? I still can't believe it!" she sobbed.

"Yes, love, I can hear you, don't cry. I will always be here for you. I'll always be with you, don't worry. Everything will be okay, I promise. All the family will be together again one day, you'll see," I replied.

This must be one of Ann's dreams, I surmised. I often wondered, in the past, whether she really spoke to her mum and dad like she said she had done in her dreams all those years ago, but now this proved it without a shadow of a doubt. I wish I had put more trust in her when we were together.

"It's wonderful here, love. Margaret was right about being able to go anywhere you want, anytime you wish.

I've seen her; I've spoken to her as well, she bounced in and out again, then shot off to Cyprus to visit all the places where we went to together on holiday, remember? She's fine; she said she'd spoken to you in one of your dreams after she died. You really can speak to us in your dreams can't you?  Bet you're thinking, 'I told you so,' aren't you? Rightly so, heh. I've seen your Mum and Dad as well. They were in your Mum's house. It was just like it used to be; the famous rose tree was still there at the side of the door, and the mark on the window sill where you put your bum through it that night. When we're together again, we'll be able to visit them and have a laugh, just like when we used to go with the kids for Sunday lunch.

"Anyway, what happened when I died? I don't remember a thing."

"John, it was just awful. You went to bed after the meal and the next thing I heard was a massive bump. When I went into the bedroom you were lying on the floor, so still and silent. You'd had a heart attack. Joe and I tried to revive you, but when the ambulance men came, they said you had gone. They said nothing could have been done to save you; it was just one of those things. The only blessing was you did not suffer; it could have been years of hospitalisation and pain I suppose, couldn't it? We are managing okay. Thanks for leaving us financially secure, by the way. I know it may sound callous, but thanks anyway. Jean and Joe and all the family were devastated when you left us. I don't think we'll ever get over it, you know. Jean's expecting

another baby by the way. She says if it's a boy she's

going to call it John after it's granddad." she went on.

I could feel my emotions welling up inside. "No," I told

myself, "I've got to stay focused; I have to remain in

contact for just a few more moments." Then she said a

strange thing.

  "There was an unusual thing happened a few months

after you died John. I received this letter from Australia.

It was from a solicitor. He said he was trying to trace the

relatives of someone who had died over there and your

name had cropped up from somewhere. He said the

man who had died was descended from some native

tribe, and he had made his money from copper mining.

His family had owned the land which was stolen from them by white settlers' years ago. The land was rich in copper and this massive mine had been set up on it. Anyway to cut a long story short, he had finally been compensated for the loss of his property, got loads of shares in this mine and finished up a millionaire. When I wrote back and told the solicitor you had died, he sent another letter saying if it was proven that you were a direct descendant of this man, your children would get your inheritance. He said he'd write back and let us know, but we haven't heard anything yet."

"I don't think you should hold your breath on that one love," I said.

"They've probably got my name mixed up with someone else from when we lived in Australia; I've not got any relatives over there that I know of," I replied.

"John, I can feel you slipping away. I think I'm slowly waking. I'm so glad we've been able to talk like this. I'm so glad you're okay. I'll see you soon love, goodbye."

"Goodbye love. Don't forget, carry on with your life and enjoy it. Tell the kids I'm thinking of them always," and with that she drifted away. I suppose she'll tell the kids about her dream, but I don't think they'll believe her, no-one ever did. "Little do they know, heh?" I thought.

I started wondering about all the people on Earth who say they can communicate with the spirit world. Some

could some be telling the truth. If I've just spoken to

someone who is obviously still alive, then why can't

others? It's not beyond the realms of possibility is it;

"No," I said to myself, "It is definitely possible that is."

 Another thing puzzled me about this conversation. I

keep coming across the subject of Australian Aborigines.

Ever since that day I sat with that group of mates in that

factory all those years ago, the same subject has

seemed to follow me around and keep raising it's head.

Why am I fascinated by these people? Why can I not

escape their clutches? Sometimes I wonder if someone

pointed those bones at me, like Aussie Bob had told me.

Maybe that's why I had the heart attack. 'Come on,

John, pull yourself together,' I thought. "Get back to

what you know you must do. There is after all, someone

you must see, and as soon as possible; but before this, I

thought, I am going to clear this up once and for all."

<u>CHAPTER 10</u>

As I lay there thinking about the recent events, I realised

one thing. Any questions I wanted answering, any

mysteries that I had in my lifetime; I could now find the

answers to. My mate Rick, Darwin and Jesus had all

helped to put together the jigsaw I had in my mind. One

question remained unanswered though, a question I

had puzzled over for many years; the story of the

fascinating Aborigines of Australia. The secrets of the

Dreamtime, and the true facts about their persecution

by the whites... and more importantly my part in all this.

But how could I find out all these answers, after all, I do not know any of these people. I have no name to focus on, no-one to call for.

As I pondered over this problem, I suddenly found myself sat on a rocky slope. A wilderness was all around me, but this was a different desert to the one where I had met Jesus. This desert was one of red soil and sand, the colour of rusty metal. Termite hills were scattered around and the odd gum tree dotted here and there. This was the Australian bush. A tall, dark semi naked man approached. His skin was almost black, glistening in the bright sunlight. His face and body were adorned with painted white stripes and dots in a familiar pattern. A big grin spread across his face as he got closer, exposing his shining, ivory teeth.

"Hi boss," he shouted.

"Who are you?" I asked wistfully.

"My name is Bahlee. I come from the Yeeman tribe in Queensland," he grinned.

"How did you know I wanted to speak with you?" I asked.

"I don't know boss, I just heard someone calling and here I am," he laughed. "Tell you what though; I feel as if we know each other somehow. Ever been to Australia before?"

"Yes, I have actually, but I didn't know any of your people while I was there," I answered.

"Well, I feel close to you in some way. I feel like we have some kind of bond," he said. "Ah well, never mind, how can I help you?"

"Well," I continued, "I have had this lifelong fascination with your people and wondered if anyone can tell me about the Dreamtime legend and the truth about your persecution by the whites? Was it really as bad as some people say?" I asked.

"It was probably worse than you can imagine. Let me tell you a little of my life and it may give you some idea," he replied.

"I lived in the eighteen hundreds. One day, around eighteen fifty seven I think it was, I and some of my friends, attacked and killed a family of whites, the

Frazer's I think they were called, at a place called Hornet Bank Station in Queensland. I know it was a terrible thing to do but we had no choice. We did it because these people had kidnapped and raped some of our women.  No police or soldiers would help us, the only way we could protect ourselves was to attack them before they attacked us again. Shortly after this fight, an Army or Policeman, I'm not sure which, called Powell, came with some others and shot and killed five of our Yeeman people. Another fourteen were shot at a place called Cockatoo.

  "Eventually, over three hundred of my people were killed, in reprisal for that one attack on those white settlers, who were murdering us anyway.

"Later, in around eighteen sixty one, I heard of nineteen whites being killed in Queensland. Within two months, one hundred and seventy Aborigines had been killed in retaliation.

"I also heard, a few years later, (around eighteen seventy three) that a whole tribe, the Guugi-Yimidhirr, were wiped out completely, because of a gold rush out at Palmer River. I lost a lot of friends and relatives in those bad years.

"These killings and murders went on for forty or fifty years. No whites were ever convicted. It got to be open sport to kill us blacks. It was even considered right to put cyanide in the meat, and arsenic in the flour to feed us, in order to kill off our troublesome tribes.

"Even in nineteen twenty eight, when two blacks from the Walbiri tribe killed a pastoralist near Coniston, Northern Territory, for abusing our women up there, police killed seventy of our people. The local Board of Justice deemed the killing of us blacks was justified.

"So you see, right up to the forties and fifties, way after my death, the persecution was still happening. Land was still being stolen, much of it holy land, essential for our way of life and our belief in Dreamtime, which is probably a good connection to the answer to your other question, I suppose."

"Yes please," I said, "I never thought things were as bad as you have just told me."

"Well you see, people have short memories nowadays; they only remember what is convenient and what they want to. Anything considered embarrassing to the Government is swept under the carpet. We will not forget though. I only hope the lessons of the past can alter the future, but while greed and jealousy thrive on Earth, I doubt whether things will change. If only people could see the future, if only we could tell them what lies ahead, it could be so different. Anyway, to carry on with your question, Dreamtime.

"The Dreamtime is the basis of all Aboriginal Society. It is the beginning, it is the beginning that never ended, a little like it is here, I suppose."

"In the beginning, Dreamtime tells us that there was nothing. The land, the sky, and all things contained therein were formed by supernatural mysterious beings. Each tribe has its own creators of the deserts, mountains, coasts etc. All these things have special Dreamtime stories, but in all of them, Land was the icon. The creators lived in the land or sky watching over us. Every hill, tree, animal or bird, every natural phenomenon, all came into existence in the Dreamtime. It was during the Dreamtime that all our laws, which must be strictly obeyed, were laid down. Laws on food distribution, marriage, and death. Rituals had to be performed, so that spirits could travel in peace to his or her spirit place.

"The creators didn't disappear, they just became invisible to us, as they hid in the trees and rock crevices, some in the air, some changed to the wind or rain, thunder and lightning, but always watching to see that we lived the correct life. Maybe Dreamtime is a little like the truth here. After all, we still don't know how the universe was formed, do we? I think, if the time comes when man could find the truth of the creation of the universe, it could well be an Aboriginal who is the one to do it. Our minds are so advanced compared to the tired, predictable, greedy westerners and whites."

"I think you could well be correct there, mate," I replied. "I only hope that in the future your minds don't become the same as ours, contaminated by civilisation. One question before you leave, which I suppose you must do soon? Were your lands seized by the whites so they could build a copper mine?" I asked.

"Why yes, I believe they were," he replied, "Why do you ask?"

"Oh, it really doesn't matter, but I think, when you meet your descendants in the future, they may have some good news for you; and you know what? I think you may be right, by saying that you feel close to me."

"Many thanks my friend. I am in no doubt that we will meet again one day. Now that we know each other we can meet again anytime one of us wants to, can't we? If there is ever anything I can do for you, please don't hesitate to ask," I said.

"Like I said before," he answered, "I feel as if we have been close before, and now that we have spoken, I know we will always be close. Until we meet again, my friend, goodbye."

With that, he rose from his squatting position, stretched his long arms above his head as if preparing for an athletic encounter and, half trotting, half walking, he faded into the hazy heat-shimmering horizon.

My thoughts turned somewhat homeward. There was someone whom I must see, and as soon as I possibly could. I must go there now.

# CHAPTER 11

As I walked up the narrow country lane, the large
willow tree swayed gently in the breeze. A slender bay
horse lifted his stooping head from grazing his lunch to
see who was approaching his field which surrounded
the tiny cottage. I immediately knew exactly where I
was as I opened the rusty old wrought iron gate. The
quaint white walled bungalow, surrounded by the
neatly trimmed hawthorn hedge, was the house where
my Mother and Father moved to after they left the
Council house of my childhood. I had lived there with
them for a couple of years before I got married. At one
time, that little two bedroom house was home to me,

my mum and dad, two brothers and a younger sister, crammed inside. For the last twenty-five years though it was just Mum, Dad and my elder brother Harry, happily living there in their own little heaven. Harry was unfortunately unable to live alone. He had a learning disability from birth, and my parents had spent almost their entire lives caring for him. They had taken him all over the world on holidays, and all lived in that secluded little bungalow, the three of them encapsulated in their own isolated world. I think when my mother died, that was why my father and brother were so devastated.

I opened the faded, green back door and went inside. I made my way towards the living room, through the passage, past the kitchen and pantry, which I noticed was stacked up with food on the newspaper lined shelves. There must have been a dozen two pound bags of sugar in there. My mum had a thing about running out of sugar. I think it came from rationing during the war.

I knew by my past experiences, exactly what to expect, and I wasn't in the least bit surprised, as I entered the room, to see everything just the way I remembered it. A small, quaint room; the dining table to one side with a white plastic cloth draped over it. The settee and two matching armchairs in the middle, strategically placed to get the best view of the TV, which was under the window so the sun never shone on it to spoil the picture. An old, cracked, tile fireplace was the focal point, a two bar electric fire in the centre. This was the beginning of the age of smokeless fuel, and there was no gas available where they lived. On the mantelpiece were a couple of photos which I recognised as me and some or my brothers and sisters when we were young. A couple of old brasses and an ornament of ceramic flowers.

As my gaze swept around the room, there sat in her favourite chair, as always, was my Mum; her glasses perched on the end of her nose. She looked beautiful, I thought. The tired, pained look that she had on her face when she was ill, had gone, and was replaced by a calm, contented expression.

"Hiyah Mum," I shouted.

She turned her head, jumping to her feet as she did so.

"I didn't know you were here," she said, somewhat surprised.

"John love, oh son, come here," she cried.

I embraced her as she gathered me up in her arms.

"Oh Mum, I have missed you so much, why did you leave us?" I said choking back my tears.

"I'm sorry son; you know I didn't want to go. I would have done anything to have been able to stay, but this tired, old body just gave up on me. I suppose it was just a case of 'my time being up.'" she stuttered. "How is everyone?  Are you all well, how's your dad and Harry and everybody?" she shouted excitedly, as if she couldn't get the words out quickly enough.

"We're all fine, mum. You have a new great granddaughter now, our Jean's little girl, Maisy. She's almost one year old now. The rest of the family are all okay.  Dad's not too good though. When you were taken from us he was shattered. I don't think he'll ever get over it, his heart is broken."

"Where is he now?" she asked.

"He managed to stay on here in the house with Harry for a couple of years, but what with his own failing health and Harry getting Parkinson's disease, he couldn't cope. He's in sheltered accommodation now and Harry's in care but don't worry, mum, I used see them every week and they are both well looked after."

"Yes, I know Harry's okay. I speak to him regularly," she said.

I had always wondered about our Harry's mental abilities. He used to say he talked to our Gran after she died. At first I thought it was his imagination, but after a few months I got to thinking that, maybe, with him having learning disability and his mind not being contaminated with the pressures of modern living, work, sex, money and all that stuff,  maybe he  could use his mental powers in a way we couldn't.

"Do you really speak to him, mum?" I asked, "I know he always used to say he talked to Gran after she died, didn't he?"

"Yes, he still does. I met her only just a while ago and she told me so. He has a special gift that lad; he's the only one I know that I can talk to easily. He's a very special lad."

"Yes Mum. Remember how, when he was younger and not affected by that terrible Parkinson's, he used to flick screws and nails up into the air with his thumb and forefinger and catch them spinning upright in the palm of his hands, both together sometimes. He used to keep them spinning for ages didn't he? We all tried but none of us could do it could we? I also remember how he never went to school but taught himself to read and write," I said.

"Yes and that's not all" she continued. "Did you know that he used to be known by all the neighbours as 'the lad who could mend broken light bulbs'? They all used to bring their dud bulbs and were amazed when he got them to light again. Don't ask me how he did it, bless him," she added.

I was beginning to realise that communication between living and (for want of a better word) dead, was by no means impossible, indeed it was probably much more common than those on earth were aware of.

"We'll all be together again one day, John. It's a wonderful place here." she said.

Mum went on to tell me how she had met her parents and made up with her Dad, my Granddad. They had had a massive row when she was a young girl, you see, and had not spoken for years. I had never seen a photo of him; she wouldn't allow any in the house, so I didn't know what he looked like as he died before I was born. I never did find out what the row was about; parents weren't as open with their children then as they are now. "I wonder what he will look like if I meet him? Another question I'll have to find the answer to eventually," I thought.

We chatted for ages about old times, and what had happened in the family since she left us. I could see by now she seemed to be getting a little tired. I think all this excitement was beginning to get the better of both of us.

"Mum, I'm going to go now, I'll see you later. You do know I love you so much don't you," I said.

"Of course I do, son," she said. "When I was in hospital those last few days, you remember, when I was in a coma?"

"Well?" I asked.

"I knew you came and sat holding my hand every night. I couldn't tell you, but I always knew you were there. Bless you son, you didn't have to come every night you know," she stuttered.

"Yes I did," I sobbed, "you are my Mum."

I could feel the warm tears rolling down my cheeks

again.

"Bye for now, Mum, see you soon!"

I made my way out of the house, turning as I walked

down the lane, to see her standing,

looking through the window. I gave her a wave and then

she disappeared.

CHAPTER 12

My eyes blinked open; I was surrounded by total and absolute darkness. Where the hell am I now, I wondered? I was suddenly having great difficulty keeping up with the pace of what was happening around me. I was just coming to terms with events and now, here I was, confused and bewildered again. Will there ever be an end to this? 'Actually, thinking about it, everyone keeps telling me there is no beginning or end to anything so who knows what will happen,' I said to myself.

The only sound I could hear was a rhythmic thumping. 'Was it my heart beating? Can't be if I'm dead,' I thought. The noise reminded me of the base of a stereo, when some boy racer pulls up by your side at the traffic lights, posing in his shining black BMW, tinted windows and radio on full blast. I felt like I was floating in water, every now and again the space around me seemed to close in; I've never experienced anything like it before.

After what seemed like hours, I noticed a small kind of orange glow appearing ahead. It slowly seemed to be getting nearer and nearer. This was completely different to what I had experienced when I died. 'Anyway,' I said to myself, 'Even I can't die twice, surely?'

Suddenly, I felt a massive shock. I was hurled forward at a tremendous pace, and thrust into the bright light of what appeared to be the outside world. I looked around frantically to find myself lying in a pool of blood, a shabby stained sheet under me. A giant pair of chunky brown hands reached down, picked me up and carried me to a nearby table. These massive hands were attached to what I first thought was a giant of a woman, who proceeded to bathe me with a warm damp towel.

 I looked down and was amazed to see this tiny little brown body, two stick like legs kicking away for all they were worth. Then I realised what this was. This wasn't death; I should have known what was happening. This was life, I was being born!

 "You have a beautiful little boy," the woman who gripped me said, to someone draped on the bed, looking exhausted. She handed me to her as she spoke.

This must surely be my mother, I decided. She cuddled me to her breast, sighing heavily and weeping tears of joy. "Thank God, thank God," she repeated over and over again.

As I gazed into her eyes I saw she was a young, beautiful girl, about twenty-five or so; long raven black curly hair, deep brown eyes, tearful but happy and a dark brown complexion the colour of rich chocolate. 'She reminds me of an Australian Aborigine' I thought, 'Yes, I'm sure she is.'

I turned my head and looked around the sparse room. Bare brick walls, hard, uncarpeted, wooden floor and an old wood burning stove in the corner. A bare, electric light bulb swung slowly in the centre of the room casting long dancing shadows on the walls. The sun was shining through a small curtain-less window in the far corner, where I could see a group of three older women huddled together, quietly whispering some secrets they obviously didn't want anyone else to hear.

One thing I couldn't quite grasp though was why, if I was a new born baby, I could understand all that was going on around me. I was contemplating this, when I noticed one of the older women leave the room hurriedly. She reappeared a few moments later accompanied by a man. He whispered something to the woman and turned to slowly approach me and my mother. He was a tall slim man, definitely an Aborigine. He wore a large, brown, bush hat which he removed as he reached us, flinging it onto the bed. I noticed how his skin was almost black but his eyes were deep gunmetal blue.

When he reached us, he leaned over and tenderly kissed the woman, whom I was now sure, was my mother, on her cheek. I presumed by now that this was my father.

"He's real small love, our lovely, precious little boy, he's so small," he said.

"I know Jim, will he be OK?" she sobbed.

"I don't know love, I hope so but I just don't know," he stuttered.

He leaned over and kissed me on my forehead. A tear slowly rolling down his unshaven cheek, and then he turned and slowly walked out of the room.

I lay there looking at my mother and trying to understand what was happening. 'If I know all these things, then it follows that I must have been on earth before,' I thought, 'But I also know of my recent experiences after death. I remember speaking to all those people in the Perihelion or heaven. The one thing they all said, Darwin, Jesus and all the others, the one thing they all emphasised, was that there could never be reincarnation of people on earth, but here I am!' As I tossed this thought over in my head, my father suddenly burst back into the room accompanied by another man.

They swiftly came to the bedside and the other man said;

   "I'm sorry Judy; you know things are not good don't you? We should really be thinking of getting you and baby to hospital as quickly as possible. He desperately needs an incubator, and you aren't too good either, are you? You've lost a lot of blood. We've radioed the flying doctor service but the plane's broken down and they can't get here. We don't have any chance of getting him and you to a hospital from up here in the bush. You both wouldn't stand the journey by car love. If we lived in the city there would be no problem but it seems nobody cares about us up here. We'll do all we can but we must trust in God."  'I suppose he must be some kind of doctor' I thought.

My father seemed very agitated, annoyed even. If only I could tell them even if the worst was to happen and we didn't make it, all would be OK in the end. If only I could speak, but of course I couldn't. I did want to pull through though; I so dearly wanted to survive so I could tell people of my knowledge. I wanted to be able to help people, to educate them about the things that must be done for the human race to survive long enough to reach the ultimate existence. I wanted to live to try and unite the nations and do whatever I could to convince people that the wealth of heaven is much more important than wealth on earth. I knew it wouldn't be easy. Maybe I would end up labelled a crank or outcast like Jesus and others, but I knew I must try.

As I realised this, I also realised something else, something that should have seemed

obvious from the start of all this. I have not been

reborn, no; I have been born one of the special people

Jesus had spoken of. I'm not John any more, I'm me. I

could feel the presence of John all around. I felt I

needed to speak to someone who could help me with

my feelings, I now know John could help me, I now

know he is up there and connected to my thoughts. If

only I could speak to him or Jesus; maybe if I

concentrate all my thoughts, I could let them

 know, maybe.

CHAPTER13

"John, John," someone called. I knew, almost instantly, what was happening, I knew someone on earth was calling to me. A new life had contacted my mind, and someone had fused with my thoughts. 'How could I automatically know this? What must I do?' I thought. 'If only I could speak to someone who may be able to help me? If only Jesus was here.'

In an instant I found myself sat on a large craggy rock. I looked around. I was surrounded by parched, barren land, and almost a complete desert encompassed me. I felt a sense of isolation creeping upon me. Then, as I squinted into the piercing sunshine, I could just make out the outline of a human figure approaching through the hazy dust. As he approached, a feeling of intense joy sprang up inside me. I was so relieved and glad, it was Jesus.

"Hello John," he said rather cheerfully, "You want my help I see."

"Yes, I do, I really do." I answered rather pathetically.

After relating all the recent events that had happened, I continued, "I can't believe what has happened? How can I have experienced my birth again? I know you said there is no reincarnation of humans and I don't think it was me being born but it was so real. It was like it was me, but also as if it was someone else at the same time. Is this connection between me and some new born child possible so soon after my own death and transformation. It all seems so strange to me."

"John, what you tell me is so exciting," Jesus said. "As you quite rightly say, reincarnation is not a possibility, however, from what you describe, there is no doubt in my mind that the connection between you and this new born child is much more than most. Much more than any I have experienced before, much more even than my own. This is so special, so precious. I feel that this may be what we; the human race has been waiting for since man evolved. This could be the salvation of mankind, the major link in the chain of man's development. When a link like you and this child occurs, it is very special. This is the first total fusion of two minds that I have ever seen. I've always known it was possible. Maybe I've always thought it could one day happen, but this is unique. What you and this child can achieve is unimaginable. You and this child are as one. Do you realise John how many special people have been killed or destroyed in the past by man's inhumanity to man before they could realise their potential."

"But this child is so fragile, so small. I really fear for his future. In the environment that it is currently in, I am fearful it will not survive. What can we do?" I asked, almost pleadingly.

"John, you have at your disposal, all the minds of every expert in his field that has ever lived. All you have to do is think of anyone or anything that could help you and you will find the answer. I must stress, John, this child must survive at any cost. I'm sure that together we can save him from its present predicament. It is the responsibility of us all."

"I don't quite know why I was chosen as this child's connection?" I asked somewhat confused. "This child was born to Australian Aboriginal parents. I'm from England, although I did live in Australia for a while. I don't have any Australian relatives to my knowledge. What do you think Jesus?"

"There is no doubt that somewhere in your past, one of your ancestors was Australian, like this child. It's the only way a connection can be made, John." Jesus answered. "It's the only explanation. Think back and maybe you will see a possibility."

"Well, I remember my mother saying I was dark skinned when I was born. She put it down to the fact that my father had just returned from India after the war. We didn't pay much credence to this theory of my mum's though. We all found it rather amusing really, because she also blamed the fact that one of my brothers had webbed toes on one foot on her being frightened by a goose when she was pregnant! Maybe there was a good reason for my dark colouring. I know something though.  Having an Australian ancestor would certainly explain my obsession with Australia when I was younger, and my fascination with the Aboriginal people while I was there and afterwards. Life certainly has a way of surprising you doesn't it. Maybe we should take more notice of these uncontrollable urges and feelings we have in our lives. Then I

remembered the letter my wife had told me about. The

one she received from that solicitor in Australia. I also

started thinking of what Bahlee had said about feeling

close to me, and how I had joked about his relatives

being somehow connected to that inheritance the letter

spoke of. Could we really have been related?

   When I think back to my childhood, I do remember a

story my mother used to tell me about her dad, my

Granddad. He was called John Mitchell, (I think I was

named John after him), but an old lady who lived in a

cottage at the end of the lane insisted on calling him

John Hodge. My mother could never find out why she

called him by that name. The Hodges, you see, was a

family who lived in the neighbourhood and were always

regarded as of doubtful heritage, so to speak. The men of the family were dark swarthy looking individuals. I suppose you could describe them as very shady types. Maybe therein lies the answer to my ancestry? Who knows? I suppose I'll never find the complete truth unless… one day when I get the time, mmm… now there's a thought.

Jesus turned to me, as if asking why I had suddenly drifted off on my personal tangent. "I'll go now and try to find some advice for you," he said. "I'll see you again as soon as I have some information, John." As he faded down the track, I wondered if we would be able to save this unique child, this dearest life, this me.

<u>CHAPTER 14</u>

Steam billowed out of the top of the frosted glass shower cubicle as if it was on fire. A tall dark-skinned, slender young man emerged from the mist, snatching a towel as he went through the bathroom door into the lounge. Drying himself in front of the tall mirror, he threw back his long, shiny black hair and pulled on his pale brown uniform. It was Jack's pride and joy that uniform. He was so proud to wear it and he had never let anyone down in their hour of need while wearing it. Going back into the bathroom, he brushed his gleaming, ivory teeth and after gulping a swift mouthful of chilled orange juice, he tucked his long hair into his pilot's cap and made his way out of the front door pulling the

insect screen closed as he left.

 Jack climbed into his battered old Ford Ute and

screeched off down the dusty road. On his arrival at the

depot, he walked the twenty-five yards or so towards

the office door, glancing apprehensively at the twin

engine aeroplane sitting on the runway, its wings tilting

gently in the summer breeze.

 He entered the reception area of the building where a

large middle aged man was sitting behind the desk,

sweating profusely in the heat of an Australian

summer's day. A large white fan oscillated to and fro on

the desk, tying to lift the piles of papers scattered

haphazardly around, but failing because they were

weighted down by half full ashtrays and cups of cold tea on dirty saucers. "Blimey mate, you really must sort this place out, you know," Jack shouted, "If the boss sees this he'll go ape."

The fat man looked up from his paperwork. "O k Jack," he muttered. "You look a bit rough, mate. Been on the grog last night? Remember, mate, never let work interfere with your drinking, or is it the other way round?" he laughed.

"Didn't touch a drop, you know we aborigines can't drink that stuff anyway. We can't take it can we? No pal, I was up awake half the flaming night. I had this real bad dream. Well not so much bad as strange really," Jack answered.

"What was that?" the fat man asked.

"Well," Jack continued, "I dreamed there was a knock on my door. When I answered it there was this guy standing there."

"Excuse me for bothering you," the guy said, "What I'm about to ask you may seem odd, but please hear me out and don't be offended."

"He was a Pommie, a bit of a gent actually, if you catch my drift." Jack said.

"Are you descended from the Yeeman tribe of Aborigines from Queensland?" he asked me.

"What do you mean? Are you taking the piss mate?" I said back to him.

"No honestly, believe it or not we're related," he said, "I too have Yeeman ancestors. Thank God that you are an Aborigine with a mind that believes in the Dreamtime and being able to talk to the dead."

"But you're a Pommie!" I shouted. "Did you say dead?"

"Yes but you'll have to trust me on this one." he answered. "What I have to say to you now is a very serious matter. It could be a case of life or death for a little new born baby and his mother, and they too are from the same ancient tribe as we are."

"What do you mean?" I asked him.

"Well, you're a pilot with the Flying Doctor service

aren't you, and your plane's out of service waiting for a

spare or something isn't it?" the guy asked.

"How the hell did you know that?" I shouted.

"Never mind that right now," he went on. "There's a

new borne baby and mother up north. It's seriously

underweight and his mum's in a bad way too. If we can

get the plane flying we could save them. What kind of

plane is it and what's wrong with it exactly?" he asked.

'This is crazy,' I thought, but as you do in dreams, I

carried on.

Well I told him the model of the plane, when it was

built and that the fault was a warning light on the

landing gear that kept flashing telling us the gear was

faulty. If we were to take off we probably wouldn't land the thing again.

"Right" said the stranger, "Give me half an hour and I'll be back," and with that he shot through down the road.

Right on time, Sure enough, there he was banging on the door again half an hour later.

"I've just been speaking to the man who designed that plane of yours, he's given me a wiring diagram to show you how you can bypass that faulty circuit which is causing the problem, take a look at it," he said.

"Hang on a mo mate," I said, "That guy's been dead for years." I answered.

"Never mind about that right now. Promise me you'll take a look anyway, won't you?" he said.

"He was almost pleading with me by now, so I looked at the diagram and it sure looked like the real thing. Yep, I thought, that may bloody work. The stranger then gave me a wave, disappeared behind the hedge, and was gone as quick as he had arrived. You know how some dreams you can remember and some you can't? Well it's strange, but I can remember every detail of that diagram just as if it was imprinted in my mind."

The fat man seemed to suddenly jump to life and become interested. "Do you know Jack, there's something funny going on here," he said, "We did have an emergency call yesterday from someone up north with a new born baby. We told them we couldn't get up there right now. We've been trying all we could to get someone else up there but we haven't managed it yet. Do you think you can still remember the diagram?"

"Well yes, every detail I think. Maybe I could give it a go." Jack answered.

Jack left the office and strode over to the hanger to see the mechanic who had been working on the plane yesterday. After being told the guy wasn't in today, Jack picked up his toolbox and made his way to the waiting plane.

Boarding through the small low door, he went to the side of the fuselage where the circuit boards were located, removed the covering panel and got to work.

After what seemed like an eternity, but was probably only a few hours, and trying to recall that wiring diagram so definitely imprinted in his mind, Jack stretched up, flexed his back muscles to ease the cramp and made his way to the cockpit. He slid into the pilot's seat and started to go through the checklist as he had done a thousand times before. He eventually reached the procedure to test the landing gear. 'Here goes,' he thought, as he flicked the switch nervously.

The radio in the reception crackled into life.

"Hi, mate, you'll never believe this. The bloody beauty. The gear seams OK now. It all checks out," Jack shouted excitedly.

"You sure mate," the fat man replied. "Don't risk it unless you're a hundred percent certain pal. No good risking the plane and you if you're not."

"Yep, I'm sure. Tell Julie to get over here pronto and tell her to bring the portable incubator with her. By the way, find out the exact co-ordinates for that call you got yesterday mate, we've got a baby to save."

<u>CHAPTER 15</u>

The night air hung heavily in the humid darkness. The crickets and cicadas were humming their melodious tunes in the background as the bright light of the large half open window shone down onto the immaculately trimmed lawns. A small fluorescent green tree frog sprang onto the window, its sucker like feet gripping tenaciously to the slippery glass as if its life depended on it. The light from the window was attracting all the nearby flies and insects and the tiny frog was hungry.

Jim turned to look at what had caused the window pane to vibrate so suddenly. It seemed to bring him back from his trance-like boredom to realty. He had been sat in the corner of that clinical white waiting room for what had seemed like hours, staring at the coffee machine next to him. He hadn't had a drink though. The machine wasn't working, but he had read the instructions a thousand times. He couldn't think of anything else to do to pass the time.

A noise behind him made him suddenly jump to his feet, the large rubber swing door opened, and a man wearing a long white coat down to his knees emerged. A mask hiding his craggy features, his short brown hair covered with a gauze hairnet.

"Mr Brown," he said rather sternly, "Would you like to come through?"

Jim followed him into the long dimly lit corridor and into a small office.

"Please take a seat," the man said. Jim had decided by now that this man must be the doctor who had been treating his wife and baby.

"How's my wife and baby boy?" Jim pleaded." Please tell me what's happening, are they all right?"

"Jim, I can call you Jim can't I?" the doctor replied, "I'm afraid I have some sad news for you. We weren't able to save your wife. I'm so sorry. She died suddenly a few minutes ago. We did everything we could. It was septicaemia, blood poisoning. Maybe if we had been able to treat her sooner… well who knows?"

"And the baby? How is he? Will he pull through?" Jim asked, tears welling up in his swollen red eyes.

"The baby's holding his own. It's too early to tell yet, but it goes without saying that we're doing all we can. The next twenty four hours will be crucial," the doctor answered.

"Can I see them?" Jim sobbed.

"Of course you can, Jim. Come follow me," he said.

They left the office and Jim was shown into a small side ward. When he entered the room he looked across at the bed where Judy, his beautiful Judy, was lying, so peaceful. She seamed asleep but he knew she was gone. A small white Bible had been placed on the cabinet at her side.

"Oh Judy," Jim cried, "Oh my lovely Judy." He leaned over her lifeless body and cradled her in his arms, tears flowing down his cheeks and dripping onto her cold lifeless face.

After a few minutes, a small, dainty looking nurse entered the room. As she approached, she said, "Would you like to see your son Mr Brown? Judy's gone but she has left you a precious little gift!  Come."

Jim didn't want to leave his wife but after a few minutes he realised the nurse was right. He rose from his slouched position and forced himself to follow her out of the room, glancing over his shoulder as he left. He wanted to be sure Judy had really died; a large part of him still didn't believe it was true.

They walked down the corridor, Jim a half yard behind the nurse, still in a half-trance. They eventually reached a door with a large sign on it saying Nursery Room, Staff and Parents only Allowed. The nurse stopped suddenly, turning to Jim saying, "Mr Brown, don't be alarmed when you see baby, all the tubes and wires do look a bit scary but believe me he is doing very well. They will be removed shortly, all being well, and with a bit of luck, we'll soon have him fighting fit again."

She pushed the buttons on the security panel and the lock clicked open. As she leaned on the heavy door it opened slowly and she led Jim into the ward. Glass cots were arranged in neat rows, dozens of little babies laid out like parcels squirming on a shelf, some sleeping, some wriggling about but most crying. "It's getting near feed time," the nurse said, smiling.

At the far end of the room, Jim saw a glass incubator positioned in the corner. As they approached, Jim saw his baby, wires attached to his chest and tubes up his nose.

"Oh my baby, my special little boy, please be strong, you must pull through, you must live for your mummy, she died to give you life, thank you Judy, thank you so much," Jim uttered.

The bleep on the machine at the side of the cot was steady and regular as Jim collapsed onto the black plastic chair at the side of the cot. He couldn't stand any more, his legs had turned to jelly and he felt exhausted.

How could his wife have been taken away from him?

Why did he and his people have to live in such a

desolate and isolated place, so far away from help? If

there is a God, how could he allow this to happen?

Surely if he existed, he couldn't take the life of a young

woman on the verge of so much happiness, whilst giving

birth to her first child. Jim wondered if he would ever

see her again. He was so scared to think of the future.

How would he cope? How would he be able to raise a

child on his own? How could he earn a living and look

after a baby at the same time? He didn't know anything

about kids. All these thoughts were whizzing around in

Jim's head; his brain felt as if it was spinning inside his

skull. One thing he had decided though; the one thing

he was so definite about. His baby would be called after

his mum, Judy; he would call the baby, Jude.

# CHAPTER 16

Through the heat haze, shimmering in the distance, a cloud of rusty, brown dust was getting closer. The deep blue Holden sedan taxi pulled up at the rusty, old wrought-iron gate. Jim dragged himself out of the passenger side-door and turned to the driver saying, "How much is that I owe you, Billy mate?"

"Ah pal, just call it fifty bucks, eh, to cover the gas. I wouldn't ask you for that if things were better and I didn't have to," the driver answered. "Will you be OK, Jim?"

"Yea, I'll be fine when I get some rest," and with that Jim swivelled around and reached for the catch on the gate, stopping to lift the lid on the black, faded old mail box, nailed onto the top of the wooden gatepost. He took out the six or seven letters without even bothering to look at them, stuffing them into his pocket as he walked up the sandy pathway which bisected the chain link surrounded garden. Actually, garden is probably not the correct description of Jim's land. It was more an expanse of withered couch-grass covered lawn. He hadn't had the time or inclination for gardening in the last few hectic weeks. As he walked up the bare pathway  towards the low, single story breeze block house, Jim remembered how he and Judy were so thrilled after they and all their friends had finished building it, their little love nest they used to call it.

He entered through the narrow, wooden door and threw his coat onto the back of the chair in the corner, the letters falling from the pocket onto the bare wooden floor. All Jim needed was rest, he thought, it had been a long tiring day, twelve hours on the train and then another couple in that dusty hot old taxi. He opened the door of the enormous white fridge. 'Damn!' he thought as he noticed the contents inside. Just a green, mouldy, half loaf of bread, a few withered vegetables and a half bottle of rancid cheesy milk. He grabbed the bottle and loaf and went out of the back door to put them in the bin outside, flicking on the electric mains switch in the power box at the side of the doorway. 'If only I'd left the damn power on,' Jim thought, but he didn't know he would be gone for so long.

He re-entered the house, walking to the large white ceramic sink and turning on the cold water tap. He left it running for a few minutes so the water could cool slightly. Reaching up to the shelf Jim grabbed a large glass, filled it with water and greedily gulped it down.

'I can't think of the future just now,' he said to himself, 'Hope nobody knocks on the door.' Not bothering to undress, he collapsed onto the bed in the corner of the room and the next thing he knew, he was waking up the next morning.

A cockerel was crowing outside greeting the new dawn, a magpie was making it's own distinctive wailing cry as Jim opened his eyes, blinking in the morning

sunshine streaming through the small window. As he

rose from the bed he noticed the letters on the floor

and reached down to pick them up. The one on the top

caught his attention; it was addressed to Mrs.J.Brown. It

brought Jim suddenly back to reality. He tore open the

long brown official looking envelope and read out aloud

its contents, it said.

*Dear Madam,*

*Could you please contact my office as soon as possible regarding the estate of the late Mr Bahlee of which we believe you may have a claim to part thereof. Further details will be provided on request.*

*Yours faithfully,*

Jim looked at the date on the top of the letter, the second of June. It was now the sixth of July. Had he really been away for so long? He hated leaving his baby in that hospital but he couldn't afford to stay off work any longer. He found it really difficult to concentrate on anything other than his baby boy right now. He looked around the room. His throat was like sandpaper. 'I'll nip to the shop for some milk and a few things,' he thought to himself.

As he approached the small wooden shack that purported to be the only shop-cum-post office within a half of a mile of Jim's home, he suddenly had the thought that he may as well use the call box to ring the number on the letter he had just read. After he dialled the number, he waited a few minutes and a woman's voice answered.

"Good morning, Mr Jackson's office," the voice said.

"Oh, hello," Jim said rather hesitantly, "I'm ringing regarding a letter sent to my wife about some possible entitlement to part of someone's estate. She was called Mrs Brown."

"Putting you through," she answered after a few moments.

"Mr Brown, Derrick Jackson, solicitor," a man said, "It's really Mrs Brown I wanted to speak to, I've been trying to contact her for a while now."

"My wife died five weeks ago and I've been away," Jim said.

"I'm so sorry to hear that, I had no Idea, please may I ask you, do you and your wife have any children?" Mr Jackson asked.

"Yes, we have a new born son," Jim said tearfully, "My wife died shortly after he was born."

"Well Mr Brown, I know this is probably a terrible time for you right now, but I must tell you your son may be in line for a hefty inheritance. If you prefer I could leave it a few weeks and we can speak again then, but I would like to finalise this as soon as possible." the solicitor said in a sympathetic albeit official tone. "The estate is of a Mr.Bahlee. You see, he died intestate which means he didn't leave a will, most unusual for a man of his standing; anyway all his estate has to be equally divided to all of his blood relatives. He never married so has no wife or children, all his brothers and sisters are deceased, and so your wife and a couple of relatives we have traced to England, stand to inherit the lot."

"How much are we talking about here?" Jim asked, "because if it's only a few hundred bucks I really can't be bothered right now mate."

"Oh no, Mr.Brown, I don't think you understand. You see Mr Bahlee was the owner of a large copper mine. It is one of the largest in Australia. Your son will be a very rich man. We expect the total to be in excess of fifty million dollars. The money would obviously have to be put into trust until he comes of age."

 The phone slipped from Jim's hand, swinging loosely from the cord. 'How could this happen now when Judy was gone?' he thought. He would gladly swap all that money and more just to have her back, how can life be so unfair?

# CHAPTER 17

An ambulance screeched to a halt outside the cream painted front of the hospital building. Two green-overall dressed paramedics leapt from the two front doors and dragged a stretcher from the back. Some poor soul lying on it moaning and groaning in what appeared to be total agony. They threw open the large, black rubber doors to the emergency entrance and dashed in, pushing the stretcher frantically down the corridor. Jim was almost bowled over as he rounded the corner, "Sorry mate!" one of the paramedics shouted. "That's fine, carry on," Jim replied, as he pushed open the door and entered the waiting room. Had it really been two months since he had sat in this same room on that dark and lonely night? He went over to the coffee machine, it was still broken.

After what seemed like an eternity, but was probably only a few minutes, a large rather buxom nurse appeared, as if from nowhere. "Mr Brown, you've come for your little Jude have you?" she said.

"Yeah, I've got the carry cot thing here, like they told me to in the letter," Jim answered.

"Come on then, follow me and I'll take you to him," she said, talking as she walked down the corridor as if time was of the essence. "We'll give you some formula milk and diapers for the journey. By the way, did anyone tell you, the pilot and girl medic from the flying doctor service have been calling in whenever they could. Every time they bring in another patient, in they pop to check how Jude is. They call him the Miracle Dream Boy. I asked them why they call him that, but they just say it's a long story and they don't really understand it anyway. The pilot has some good news for you actually. He's fixed it so that he can take you and Jude home later. I'll give him a call in a minute to tell him you're here. Jude is doing really well now; you won't recognise him when you see him."

The door to the ward opened slowly, and, through the transparent sides of his glass cot, Jude saw his father hurriedly approaching. A large grin spread across his face almost cheek to cheek. The nurse leaned over into his cot to arrange the cover which he had great delight

in kicking off at every opportunity.

"You know Mr Brown," she said, "He's a really clever

little boy. If I didn't know any better, I'd swear he knows

every word I say to him."

Jude said to himself, 'It's probably a good thing she

doesn't know what I'm thinking right now,' as she

leaned over him exposing her ample cleavage. 'I think

John must have had a thing about large breasts when he

was alive and I've inherited it. Strange how he never

mentioned it over the last couple of months, mind you

the subject of bosoms had never come up I don't think'

Jude thought. They had been in contact almost

continuously since he had been born really. John had

told him of all his experiences and how they had been selected to be joined in thoughts. The people he had met since his passing, his lessons from Jesus and Darwin. Jude thought that he was almost as bewildered as John. There was so much they still didn't understand.

"Come on my little beaut," Jude's father whispered in his ear, as he leaned over and lifted him from the cot. He rocked him to and fro as he said, "You know you are the gift from Judy to me, and her gift to you is life, and enough money to live it any way you choose, I wish you could understand me, my son." If only Jude could find a way to tell him he did.

"How do you mean Mr Brown?" the nurse asked.

"Well baby Jude has inherited a lot of money, more money than we could ever have imagined. It's my wife's dying gift to him, God bless them both," he stuttered. "If only baby Jude could understand me, but he will one day."

Jude tried to smile at his dad, but he didn't see him though. If only there was a way he could make his dad see he did understand. Come to think of it, even if there was, would it be wise to let him know? How would he cope with all this, after what he's been through over the last few months? 'It's taking me all my time to cope with it all.' Jude thought to himself. 'How will I be able to live my life knowing all I do about what John has told me? Do I tell anyone? Who would believe me anyway? How will I cope with being a millionaire, when John has told me money is of no importance?" Jude could feel all these doubts welling up inside his head. He needed to speak to someone who could help him. He felt really scared now that he was about to enter the outside world for the first time. 'I have to speak to John urgently. I must call to him. John, John,' he shouted inside his head.

# CHAPTER 18

I sat bolt upright when I heard the call inside my head. 'John, John,' someone was calling. It was strong and familiar and the voice had a kind of urgency to it. As I opened my eyes and looked around the room in the dim light, I got the distinct feeling this place was familiar to me. 'I'm sure I've been here before,' I said to myself. I looked down, noticing I was in a bed, a somewhat old fashioned bed at that. You don't see flock mattresses around much nowadays, do you? On the bedside cabinet was an old fashioned clock. I peered through half-open eyes and was just able to make out the hands pointing to the time, eight-forty five it said. A cold cup

of tea was sitting on a flimsy coaster; a skin had formed

on its surface as if it had been left on the Marie Celeste.

As I lay there in a confused state, the bedroom door

creaked open, a face poked through. A friendly

comforting face. A face topped with hair curled around

plastic rollers which were covered with the traditional

hairnet. It was my mum; spectacles perched on the end

of her nose, just as I remembered her all those years

ago.

"John, John, come on lad, hurry up, you'll be late for

school if you don't get up now!" she shouted.

"Oh damn, after all that," I shouted out, "This hasn't

been another flaming dream, has it?"

My mother's face changed to a cheeky grin. "No lad, I don't think so" she said most assuringly. "There's someone here to see you," and she pushed open the door.

I was amazed. It certainly wasn't a dream, because there stood Jesus. What a wonderful sight. I didn't really know whether I was glad all I had experienced over the last period of time was real, or whether I was sad not to be still alive. 'What a dilemma,' I thought to myself.

"John, I see you have had what we call a flashback. Don't worry, you'll get used to it. I'm sure you'll have many more in times to come. I have come to see you because of my concern over your sibling on earth, Jude. You do realise he's twenty one today don't you?"

"How can he be that old?" I asked. Oh, nice to see you again by the way. How could all that time have passed so quickly? I don't seem to have been here more than a few days."

"I thought you might ask me that, John, so I took the opportunity to have a chat with someone for the best way to explain it. I asked Einstein. He would have come himself but he is busy with another newcomer right now. Anyway, this is what he said."

"Years ago, when he was on earth, he put forward the theory about the speed of light. Nothing could travel faster than the speed of light. Imagine if you could travel faster, you would be able to go to another planet and look back at the earth and see it thousands of years before you left. If you returned at the same speed you left, that is faster than the speed of light, you would arrive back on earth hundreds perhaps thousands of years before you departed. That would be impossible because you wouldn't have been born then. You can't exist before you are born and then be born again, can you? Well, if the speed of light is so final and powerful, what about the power of gravity. Gravity was thought to be the most powerful force in the universe, but if the Sun, which holds the Earth in its gravitational grip, was to disappear instantaneously, would the Earth and all the other planets in the solar system spin off before you saw the sun wasn't there? Another problem; if for instance, you were to jump off a tall building or cliff top, if gravity is the most powerful force in the universe, you should not stop when you hit the ground. You should

continue until you arrive at the centre of the earth,

shouldn't you, but some other force stops you doesn't

it?"

  "I don't understand what you are trying to say, Jesus;"

I interrupted. "What has all this got to do with time?"

  "John, what I'm trying to explain to you is this; time is

just another dimension, as is light and gravity. We

humans don't yet understand the forces of the universe;

we don't see the powers of total energy, and time on

earth is something we have invented to try to explain

something we can't understand. What may seem like

years on earth, may be just the blink of an eye,

somewhere else. The fact remains, it is twenty one

years today since Jude was born, which brings me to the point of why I'm here. John, I'm worried about what may happen, Jude is a wonderful boy and his thoughts are pure and true, but in the corrupt and dangerous world he lives we must try to help him avoid the pitfalls which will confront him now he is of age to make his own decisions. I don't want the same to happen to him as befell others. Look what they did to me if you want an example of what can happen."

"I understand what you say, but how can we help. We are up here and he is alone down there?" I asked.

"He may be alone in body, but we are only a thought away. Always be aware of his thoughts. Try to introspectively influence him to be wary. Any action he takes must be prudent and cautious. He will have many dangers to face as he goes about his tasks to resolve his and mankind's future. Please John, don't fail him or humanity."

'This is going to be one hell of a time', I thought. 'Funny though, I felt exhilarated and excited at the prospect of what lay ahead. In a strange way I was looking forward to the cut and thrust of helping a life again. I suddenly felt almost human, almost a living spirit, almost alive!

# CHAPTER 19

Jude dragged a razor over his fluffy stubble. He only shaved once a week and he didn't really have to do it that often. His dad always said he could save himself a lot of bother if he got the cat to lick it off for him. Jude really missed his dad; it had only been two months since Jim, his dad, had died suddenly from a massive heart attack. He always thought his dad never really recovered from the day Judy, Jude's mum, died shortly after giving birth to him; not that his dad ever once indicated his sorrow. He was a very devoted father,

Jude loved his dad to bits but deep down he knew Jim's heart was broken the day his mum died.

Jude and his dad were so looking forward to this day; they had talked of nothing else for months. It was Jude's twenty first birthday, the day he became a man. The day when Jim was supposed to hand over control of all the assets from the inheritance Judy had unknowingly left to her son and heir. Jim had been appointed executor of the estate when his wife had died. 'What a pity she never even got to know about the fortune she inherited before she died,' Jim had regularly said. 'If only the notification had come through a few months earlier, maybe she would have still been alive now? Who knows?'

As Jude strode out of the ornate bathroom and into the lounge, he said to himself 'What a beautiful house this is. Mum would have loved it here, I reckon.' His dad had often told him of the hard times on that Aboriginal reserve up north, where Jude was born. No jobs and no money, but Jim had always said how happy they were. Funny, Jude thought, how people can suffer adversity and hardship but still remain happy. Does money make you happy? No, because it's the fear of losing it and the possessions it buys that kills any joy the money can bring.

John had taught him all these things as he grew into adulthood. Since his birth Jude had been aware of John's presence; they were soul mates. It was like the experience of loving someone; you can't prove its there, but you know it's real.  Jude and John were joined in spirit, they were almost as one.

 When he had died and journeyed through the Perihelion, or after life, meeting anyone he wanted to, going anywhere he wished, John passed on all the knowledge he had gained directly to Jude, but Jude couldn't tell anyone about it. He had once tried to explain things to his dad, but Jim didn't understand. 'You are blessed with a vivid imagination son,' Jim had once said. "You're a clever lad, Jude, but you don't half go on a bit, son." His dad really did think he was a gifted boy, which he certainly was in his own special way.

 Jude and his dad had built this house after they had received the inheritance from one of Judy's distant relatives." Where did all this money come from?" Jude had once asked his dad.

 "It came from one of your mum's relations son," Jim replied. "In the old days many native Aborigines had their land stolen by the whites. After many years fighting through the courts, the Government decided to compensate some of them. It just turned out that your mum's relative owned probably the richest land in Queensland. It was filthy rich in copper, and he was filthy rich in money when the cash came through. Anyway, he took control of the mines, and when he died intestate, without leaving a will, the lot was divided between you and a couple of poms whom we don't really know. They took the cash and we took the mines.

When you're twenty one, son, you'll have to keep me in

the way I've become used to you know,' he often joked.

Today was that day, but money and wealth didn't

really interest Jude, only what he could do with it, was

of interest to him.

As he strode through the enormous lounge

surrounded by beautiful furniture, polished wood floors,

expensive ornaments and aboriginal artefacts hanging

on the walls, Jude remembered how his dad had told

him how they had built most of the house together,

along with the help of a few friends. Jude remembered

how they worked long and hard. It was a task of

pleasure, really, but Jim used to crack on he had done it

himself because Jude was only a small boy at the time;

but Jude knew how he had helped in his own little way.

When it was finished, all the locals called it Southfork

because it so much resembled the ranch house on

Dallas. Yes, it was that grand.

Jim had never let money, or the love of it, rule his

head and he had made sure Jude did the same. He

always remembered his roots. There were three

Aboriginal gardeners, two chauffeurs, two cooks, three

cleaners, as well as all the workers in the mines; in fact

any Aboriginal that Jim could find work for, got a job, as

well as many whites also. Jude thought how much his

dad would be sadly missed by so many folk, but none

more so than himself. Jude had adored his dad but in

the corners of his mind he found comfort in the

knowledge they would be together again one day. There

was no doubt in his mind of that, not after what John had taught him.

Jude opened the large, heavy, carved oak front door; his Bentley was just pulling up outside, the dark blue paintwork and chrome glistening in the bright sunlight. The car door opened and the chauffeur, Jack, a tall middle aged man, eased himself out, a broad grin stretched across his swarthy face, a cheeky glint in his eye.

"Hi Jude," Jack said, "Today's the big day eh lad."

"Morning, Jack," Jude replied, "Come in for a sec will you? I want a word before we go to the solicitors."

Jack followed Jude into the lounge, "Want a drink?" Jude asked.

"Just a juice, please," Jack answered.

As Jude passed him a glass of fresh orange, he said "It sure doesn't seem like twenty one years ago since you saved my life does it, mate? If you hadn't mended that plane in time and got me and my mum to that hospital, I wouldn't have made it would I?"

Jack was the pilot for the flying doctor service who got the plane fixed and rushed Jude and his mum to the hospital that unforgettable day.

"Its not me you should be thanking mate. It's your friend up there in the Perihelion, in heaven, who told me in that dream how to fix the plane. He's the one you should be thanking." Jack enthused.

"Yes, I know all that, but if you hadn't had the courage and belief to go for it; if you hadn't had the faith in our Aboriginal religion to take a chance, nothing would have happened. Jack, I owe you my life and I'll never forget that." Jude said passionately.

"I'm only sorry we couldn't save your mum as well, she was so young, what a terrible waste of a life." Jack said.

"Thanks Jack. Anyway I've asked you in to tell you something. When I get control of my estate later, I've decided what I intend to do. I can't justify my keeping all the money while at the same time preaching to anyone who will listen that money is of no importance in our lives; and how we must work to the goal of eventually achieving equality for all the peoples of the world, just the same as we will all be equal after death; so I've decided I shall give it all to charity. Don't worry though, I intend to make sure you and all the people employed by the business will be looked after."

"I'm sorry to interrupt you, Jude, but I don't want your money, mate," Jack jumped in. "Your dad and I spoke about this day shortly before he died. I think he had inkling you may say that, anyway he asked me to tell you that if anything happened to him, I should tell you how he felt."

"What did he say?" Jude asked.

"He told me to ask you to think very carefully about what you intend to do in the immediate future and not to make any rushed decisions. He was a very astute

man, your dad. He and your mum had a real hard time

up north when you were born, and he didn't suffer fools

kindly. He said for you to imagine you were driving

down the highway when you noticed a dishevelled,

scruffy, bushman or tramp, standing on an old soapbox

at a street corner. He is preaching that he knew what

was going to happen when we die, and how he was

going to make the world a better, safer place to live, a

world where everyone will be equal and where all

religions will be united to believe in the 'ultimate

existence'. What would be your reaction, or more

importantly, what would be the reaction of most

people? Most would probably think, 'Here we go again,

another old crank, or maybe another wino trying to make an easy buck.'

   "Then, imagine, if you arrive home from work one day, you switch on the TV and there on the screen is a dapper, young guy dressed in a smart suit, proposing a well planned and expertly prepared argument, put forward by a respectable political party with a manifesto for dramatic change, backed by the power money can buy from the media; enough money to see through what they start."

   "Who do you think people will take most note of? Who do you think stands the greater chance of success? Which will do most to influence society, the bushman whose ideals are without question correct, or the one who recognises the society he lives in and uses all his assets and strengths to their greatest effect and potential? That's what your dad asked me to say, Jude; the rest is now up to you mate."

"But what about you, Jack. What do you think? What's your personal opinion?" Jude asked.

"My opinion is of no consequence, Jude. You must do what your head and more importantly your heart tells you to do; but remember, anything you want from me, just ask. I'll back you all the way. I'll always be here for you sport; I'll never let you down."

Jude looked up at the shiny brass plate on the office door. 'D. JACKSON' 'Solicitor and Commissioner,' it read. He pushed open the door and went inside.

"Good morning Mr Brown," the attractive dainty brunette said as she rose from her desk. "I'll tell Mr Jackson you're here."

He was immediately ushered into the inner office where he was welcomed by its incumbent, a small, neat man with thinning grey hair and thick, black-rimmed glasses, who looked more like a family doctor than a solicitor.

"Good morning, Jude," I hope you are well?" he said. "I have all the documents prepared and ready for your signature."

As Jude sat back in the plush leather chair, Jack's words of earlier that day were still revolving around his head. He hadn't said anything, but he had known what his father's wishes were, long before Jack had told him. He had spoken to his dad soon after he died, in one of his frequent dreams. Now he knew exactly what he must do.

"After I sign the forms, I want you to do a few things for me, please. I want you to draw up a contract to appoint Mr Jack Dawson as my representative to manage all my business affairs; and I want you to make enquiries about what needs to be done in order to set up a new political party!"

<u>CHAPTER 20</u>

"Dad, what was that guy called who was a distant relative of granddad Lynch, and who inherited that copper mine here in Queensland?" the young girl sitting in the armchair, asked. The question came from Cherie, Joe's daughter and John's beautiful little granddaughter.

"His name was Jude Brown. Why do you ask?" Joe answered.

"Well, there's an advert here in the paper for a new political party. It's very strange but very interesting in its own way," she said. "It says, 'Do you think God is alive in heaven? Do you believe in the equality for all people on Earth, and are you fed up with the greed and lies of politicians? If your answer to any of these questions is yes, call us now. The Universal People's Party. Proposed by Mr. Jude Brown.'

Cherie was nineteen, an impressionable age. A slim, attractive young girl, dark skin and bright blue eyes, just like her mother. She had inherited all the good points of her mother who was a native Australian, and her dad Joe, who although born in Australia when John had lived there, had actually been raised in England. He had satisfied his unquenchable desire to return to his land of birth, and had met and married Cherie's mother and settled in a small town called Ipswich, near Brisbane, Queensland. Tragically, Sally, Cherie's mother, had been killed in a car crash almost ten years ago. Cherie was only nine years old. The whole family was almost wiped out on that terrible, frightening day, but Joe and his

daughter had miraculously survived. The accident had

left Cherie severely traumatised. She suffered from

flashbacks, and some form of schizophrenia, a kind of

loss of contact with reality, and hearing voices in her

head. At least that's what the doctors had diagnosed.

She hadn't been able to tell anyone before, about the

voices she had heard occasionally in her head since she

was born. After she was hospitalised and given

medication, the voices had stopped. She now lived an

unspectacular life, and had balanced her feelings and

health to a stable, boring normality. Her main interest in

her life was an obsession with her mother's Aboriginal

culture. It seemed to satisfy her anxiety and strong

feelings of distress caused by the trauma she had as a

child. She didn't tell her dad, but later that afternoon she rang the number in the advert.

It seemed ages since she had rang the number in the paper. Cherie had been waiting eagerly for some response. She began to wonder if there had been any real reason to make her enquiry at all. Maybe it had all been some kind of wind up.

The doorbell rang; Cherie jumped up with a start and skipped over to the door. When she opened the door she saw the postman standing there, dripping wet from the unseasonable downpour.

"Package for you, love," he said in a pleasant tone as he handed her the large brown, foolscap envelope.

"Thank you," she said as she closed the door, and wandered slowly over to the chair in the lounge. She opened the package to find a thick booklet. On the first page it said, "THE MANIFESTO OF THE UNIVERSAL PEOPLE'S PARTY." Over the next few days, Cherie eagerly read every letter, sentence and page of that booklet; she couldn't put it down for more than a few minutes at a time. It was as if the person who wrote the words she so avidly read, was doing so while talking to her in person. As if they were together in the same room, and had known each other for years. Their thoughts were certainly on the same wavelength, so to speak. She was enthralled, no, more than that, she was captivated. Even more so, when she realised that the local Party Office address was in Brisbane city, just an hour away on the train. She couldn't travel by car after her terrible accident, in fact just the thought of getting into a car sent shivers running down her spine and brought her out in a cold sweat. The article in the manifesto which interested her most of all, was titled 'Social Security'. It read as follows:

'The goal of this Party is not to promote Communism or Marxism or for that matter Socialism. Communism (or in its original true form, Marxism) has many favourable policies to promote the equality of man. Unfortunately the one thing it does not take into account, is the aspect of giving an individual the incentives that a Capitalist society offers, i.e. the prospect of attaining wealth and gaining power. No Country or Government could possibly hope to achieve the total equality of its population, when the main

incentive for people to work harder, and further their

careers is purely financial gain. Ask yourself, does a

sportsman or woman play his or her favourite game

purely for the financial rewards it may bring, or because

he or she loves to participate in something they enjoy

doing? Surely if the answer was financial gain and

nothing else, then there would be no amateur

sportsmen and women; no voluntary unpaid social and

medical workers, etc. If you need an example to qualify

my point, then I suggest we need look no further than

the most dedicated, loving person the world has

possibly ever known, Mother Teresa of Calcutta. This

party is convinced that, if someone follows their chosen

trade or profession because they love what they do,

they would be of much greater value to society and themselves, than someone who does the same for financial gain alone. This must take into account the premise that we may all attain a decent standard of living and appreciate a reward for working harder than the norm, without the expectation of amassing the obscene wealth, as some are allowed to do today.

'We realize that it would be virtually impossible for any country or government to implement any policies to achieve this kind of equality. For one thing, they would probably be voted from power in a democratic society, where the minority of the population possesses the majority of the wealth. These same people would quickly remove their investments to a more favourable economy at the first sign of a downturn in the profitability of their capital. Look at what has happened in Countries like The Soviet Union, China and Cuba and any other non-Capitalist economy. No, the only possible way the policies we propose, for the equality of all Mankind, can be achieved, is on a Global scale, not unilaterally. Every government in the world must have identical policies. Indeed we must advocate going one step more. There can only be one government in the world, one party in the world, and that party must be our party; The Universal People's Party.'

 'These changes will not be popular in today's social climate. No wealthy individual will relish giving up part of their riches or power when some have worked hard and long to achieve it, although many have attained their wealth and power simply by a fortunate, privileged birth. Unfortunately, it's a tiny minority of the World's population that control its wealth, and ultimately, it's power. Indeed if it was the opposite, then maybe we would not have the catastrophic problems which we are so fast approaching. It will take many years, hundreds, possibly thousands to achieve our goals. Most reading this article at the time of publication, may not see the fruits of their labours, but rest assured, as the human race continues to rape and plunder the very planet to which it owes it's existence, man will eventually realise that the policies of this Party are the obvious, and indeed the only, future for mankind. There will be no choice!'

Cherie was convinced. She must ring or contact Jude right now. At this time, she obviously she had no idea of the strange cognitive minds of Jude and her granddad,

John, but she knew she must call. She reached for the

phone and started to dial the number at the top of the

paper.

## CHAPTER21

Jude was sitting in his sumptuous black leather chair, sipping a cup of coffee, and staring aimlessly out of the gallery-style window overlooking the splendour of Moreton Bay and the busy extravagant harbour of Brisbane Marina, when the phone suddenly rang. It brought him back to reality from his daydreaming. He lifted the receiver to hear the squeaky voice of Jane, his secretary. "Mr Brown, I have a call from a lady who asks to speak to you. She says she's related to you. Are you in or out?"

"Yea its o.k. Jane, put her on," Jude replied. "All I need now is another crank trying to screw me for money; still it may be good for a laugh."

"Mr Brown?  Hello, I'm sorry to trouble you in your office; I suppose you're very busy?" Cherie said. "I've just read your Party Manifesto you sent to me and I felt I must ring you. I believe you and my Father are related distantly. I think your father is related to my Grandfather, his name was John Lynch. Does that ring any bells?"

The phone almost slipped from Jude's grasp as he jumped bolt upright in his seat. He obviously knew he had some distant relatives. His dad had told him of them when the legacy of his estate had been decided, but he never dreamed he would ever have any contact with them. To the best of his knowledge they were all living somewhere in England. The prospect of meeting any of his relatives frankly scared him to death. 'What would happen if they discovered I was in contact with John? Could she know? Why else would she

236

ring? What could I say? All these questions ran simultaneously through Jude's head, he was dumbstruck.

"Hello, Mr Brown, are you still there?" Cherie asked.

"Yes, yes I'm still here. I'm sorry; you took me a little by surprise." Jude answered, deciding to play it cool. "How can I help you?"

"My name is Cherie, Cherie Lynch, my dad Joe is John's son. John inherited part of the same estate that you did I believe. Like I said, I've just read your Party Manifesto. The part I was particularly interested in was the Social Security bit, and I would like to join your party. Would that be OK?"

"That would be more than OK, that would be great." Jude replied, becoming a little more confident with the friendly, cheerful voice on the other end of the line. "Where do you live Cherie?"

"Quite close actually, near Ipswich. How do I go about joining?" Cherie asked inquiringly.

"Well, if you would care to, I would really like to meet you and your father. How would it be if I came around to your place and brought the party info with me?"

"OK, but I'll have to clear it with dad first, I'm sure he'll be cool though. I'll ring you later and fix up a date that's convenient." She said.

"Fine, look forward to it," Jude replied, "Bye for now."

Jude's heart was racing. He felt exited and somewhat apprehensive at the same time, but he knew it's what he had to do. Somehow he felt like part of the Lynch family, it just felt right.

It was a few days later, when Jude found himself driving up the long winding hill to Joe and Cherie's neat little low set bungalow. His heart was throbbing in his chest and he took a long, deep drag on his cigarette, a habit he had been trying to give up for years but had failed miserably to do. Suddenly, there it was. Number 100 painted in large white numbers on the solitary black letter box which sat on a pole at the side of the road. He jumped out of the limo and strode quickly up the dusty path. As he approached the bright yellow door opened slightly, to reveal Cheri's pretty, cheeky face smiling broadly through the fine mesh fly screen panel, her white teeth glistening in the sunlight.

Jude had never really had much time for the opposite sex. Sure there had been the odd date, after all, there was never going to be a shortage of girls willing to go out with a wealthy, good-looking young millionaire bachelor, but he had never experienced the feeling he got when his eyes met Cherie's. 'If ever there was such a thing as love at first sight,' Jude thought,' if this isn't it, then it must be pretty close.' He was well and truly smitten.

 As they chatted over a cup of coffee in the lounge, just the two of them, as Joe had been called away unexpectedly, Cherie told Jude about the accident and how her Mother had been tragically killed when she was just a young girl. Jude told how he also had lost his mum shortly after he was born. The conversation somehow swung around to how Cherie had been so deeply affected by her Mum's death, and she inadvertently mentioned how she had heard voices inside her head telling her how everything would be all right. It was strange how she felt she could tell Jude all these private and personal feelings without any embarrassment, she thought, as if she had known him all her life. It was only after Cherie's apparent trust in him; when Jude, for no apparent or logical reason, suddenly and totally out of the blue, decided to dramatically disclose his own feelings. He had been waiting for this moment all his life. Someone whom, for no reason at all, he felt he could reveal his inner self to.

"You know how you said you heard voices inside your head, and how they stopped when you took the medication the doctors gave you, well Cherie, and I've never told this to anyone before, you may not believe me, but I too, hear voices. Have you heard of the Dreamtime, because if you have you'll know what I'm talking about? You'll know how we Aboriginals can communicate with our ancestors in our dreams. Do you believe Cherie?"

"Yes, Jude, I do. Carry on."

"Well, you may not believe, but some can speak to relatives outside of dreams, in consciousness."

"How do you know that?" Cherie asked excitedly. "Are you telling me you are one of these people?"

"Yes Cherie, I don't quite know why I'm telling you all this, but that's what I'm saying."

Cherie wasn't surprised by Jude's revelations. She almost knew what he was about to say each time he spoke, but she wasn't expecting what came next.

"Cherie, I know your Granddad John; Like I said before, I've never told anyone this before and if you don't believe me I wouldn't blame you at all. If I've offended you in any way, please tell me and I'll leave."

"How do you mean?" Cherie queried. "I don't understand, you can't have met him. He died way before you were born. Oh my God, are you saying what I think you're saying?"

"I've never met your Granddad John; you know what I'm trying to tell you don't you?  I know him from speaking to him in my mind, our thoughts are intertwined, and we speak constantly. I know it's hard to believe, but there, I've told you now. Do you think I'm crazy? I wouldn't blame you if you did; sometimes I even think I am myself."

"No, I don't think that at all," Cherie said somewhat sympathetically. I was only ten years old when I started my medication, but even then, I suspected I didn't really need it. I never thought I was ill or crazy, like you just said, but at that age when doctors tell you to do something, you just think they know what's best, don't you?"

"Cherie, please let me prove my sincerity?" Ask me something. Yes that's it; ask me something about your Granddad John that no-one could possibly know; some intimate personal secret only he would know."

"I don't know what to ask," Cherie replied a little perplexed, "but I know someone who would, you just hang on for a moment."

Cherie reached over and gently lifted the cordless phone from its holder, dialling the number as she walked over to the sofa at the other side of the room.

"Gran, hi, it's Cherie, are you OK?"

After a short conversion with her Gran, John's widow, Cherie walked back to where Jude was sitting.

"She was a little confused," Cherie said as she delicately replaced the receiver, "but she's given me something to ask you, something that she says no-one could possibly know other than her and John. If you answer this then you must be for real. Gran said that when she and John were younger, when they first started going out together, she made a request for a record to be played on a local radio station. It was at Christmas time, and she dedicated it to John for a laugh. She never expected it to be played, but it was. They always called it their special record. What was it Jude? What was that special record?"

Jude thought for a few moments, concentrating, focusing his mind, and then he turned to Cherie, slowly looking into her eyes.

"If I tell you the answer, then will you believe me Cherie?" he said hesitantly.

"If you know this Jude I will have no alternative will I? She replied.

"Alright then. The record was called 'Gimme Some Loving' by The Spencer Davis Group," he shouted abruptly.

"How did you do that? How the hell did you know? You really are telling the truth, aren't you? You sure are for real Jude." She said jumping around uncontrollably.

"Cherie, our thoughts are so precious, so private, and so important. If you have any doubts over your need for medication, then maybe you should think again. Don't forget that any time, in the Bible, or any other religion for that matter, which someone has told of speaking to their God, it was always in a dream or thought. No-one has ever physically met or seen their God, or deceased relative in the flesh, have they? Maybe your thoughts could help you come to terms with your life, your real thoughts I mean, not those controlled by medication. I only make these suggestions as a possibility; you understand Cherie It could be that the Doctors are right in your case. I don't know, all I ask is that you think about it. The decision must be yours at the end of the day. I'm sorry Cherie but I have to rush off now," Jude said as he glanced down at his wristwatch, "I have a prior appointment in an hour. May I ring you later?" he asked as he walked out of the door.

"Yeah, please do Jude; Dad will really want to meet you when I tell him what happened here today. I would really like to meet you again as well." Cherie said rather coyly.

After Jude had left, Cherie thought long and hard about what had happened over the last few hours. Had it been hours or minutes, she thought. It had seemed like seconds. She stared at the forms on the coffee table. She picked up the top copy and looked intently at the heading, 'The

Universal People's Party'; she reached excitedly for the pen.

As Jude drove off down the road towards the main highway,

he began to wonder if what had happened to Cherie could

have happened to others. Was it possible that more people

diagnosed with schizophrenia or other mental disorders

could have been denied reaching their potential by the

administration of drugs and other treatments? What would

they have done to him if he hadn't had the advice to keep

quiet about his experiences? What would modern-day

society have done to Jesus or other so called prophets? He

began to feel vulnerable, now that he had told someone else

of his innermost feelings, but he was sure he could trust

Cherie. 'No, she wouldn't let me down would she? He

thought to himself.

<u>CHAPTER 22</u>

_Two slender fingers and a matching thumb folded around the shiny brass door handle slowly revolving it half a turn clockwise. The heavy solid oak door creaked open and a tall slender, somewhat elegant young man entered the room. He was dressed in a fashionable, light grey suit, very trendy, not at all like the other dour, grey men seated around the massive polished square oak table. He strode over arrogantly, to the one vacant chair, sat down and diligently rearranged the nameplate in front of him four inches to the left. Everything had to be just perfect. He reached down into his large black leather briefcase and extracted a red folder, placing it carefully on the table.

"I presume we have all read the document up for discussion gentlemen, so let us consider the serious implications of it," he rasped. "Look if you will at the introduction marked Monetary Policy of this so called Universal People's Party. I will read a section and then you may like to offer your comments."

He rose quickly, as if in a hurry to complete his speech, then continued.

"It starts, and I quote, 'For how much longer can the human race continue on its self-destructing financial journey? How can we justify so few having so much, while so many have so little?' The message to everyone in the wealthy Western capitalist economies must be to look up from burying your heads in the sand. You cannot ignore what's happening forever because forever simply doesn't exist on Earth. The end will come quickly enough without us accelerating it by continuing on our current path.

'Ask yourselves, if a sportsman or woman earns millions of pounds or dollars, where does this money come from? If a president or politician or even a local representative is paid thousands or millions where does that money also come from? There can only be so much wealth in the world. It can only be derived from one source. One man's gain is another man's loss. Surely if a limit was set on any one individual's wealth, then there would be more for others. If businesses were limited to the amount of wealth they could accumulate, and if massive international conglomerates were owned and controlled by one Governmental Body, then surely there would be more money available for the benefit of all. I, as head of this party, am not an economist, but can anyone tell me that I am wrong? Anyone with a conscience, that is.

'As stated elsewhere in this document, no single Government of any one country could hope to achieve success with the policies based on the previously mentioned beliefs. If they were not ridiculed by the all powerful media they would soon be voted out by the population who are influenced and yes even controlled by it. The old expression 'The pen is mightier than the sword' is even truer when the pen is supplemented by radio, TV and even the internet. The only possible recipe for success is to envelop the World with one policy, one Government, one Party, our Party.

'The Global Party can still respect the democratic rights of every individual in every nation. Local elections can still be held to select local representatives. But every country must have equal rights within the Central Government.

Any Country or Government that refuses to join this Global movement must not be allowed to jeopardise our success.

We are not advocating aggression; we are stating quite categorically that we, as the population of this planet, do not have the luxury of time for us to fail. There must be constant and vigorous monitoring of every country's finances. Audits must be regular and thorough. Any individual discovered to be abusing their positions must be dealt with swiftly and severely until the message becomes clear to all, as it eventually will, that if they cheat, they do not just cheat on others, they cheat on themselves. Our children, and all that follow, will look back in history to this time, and decide whether this was the birthday of true democracy or the beginning of the end. We cannot fail them.

'We must halt the senseless wasting of crucial irreplaceable resources on pointless expenses; wars, weapons, and the pathetic attempts to explore our insignificant Solar System. All our investment in science must be targeted towards the goal of all life, the attainment of the ultimate existence in paradise, in Heaven. We alone, can attain these heights; we can succeed, but only together, only as a nation of one, only as a Global unified race.'"

The young man slumped to his seat as if exhausted mentally.

"This document disgusts me" he uttered. "How can anyone be so naïve? Listen to what follows, this really cracks me up.

"This section goes on to speak of limitations of wealth. It advises that no individual will be allowed to hold assets over a specified figure. It advises a sum of Five million pounds sterling or its equivalent to begin, reducing over a period of twenty years. It also advises what amounts to the nationalisation of all major industries, even the Banks, all to be run by a so-called Central Global Body. How can this possibly work? This guy lives in a fantasy world, he's insanely naive. This man Brown is causing serious concern."

At this juncture an older, slightly balding man raised his hand as if asking his schoolteacher for permission to speak.

"Yes Harold, what have you to say?" the young man asked.

Harold stood, adjusting his red and grey striped tie, as if trying to free his vocal chords.

"Don't you think that if left to their own devices this party will eventually fizzle out as others have done in the past? Look what happened to communism in the seventies and eighties?" Harold said, looking rather pleased with his contribution to the debate.

"No, unfortunately not," the younger man answered. "The popularity of this so called People's Party is growing daily. It's already conquered Asia and Africa, many far Eastern countries seem to be going the same way, and we've all seen how fast its popularity is growing in the West. They've gained many seats on the local Government scene. How long before they make gains in Parliament. If we don't appear to be actively opposing this destruction of our society, how do you think other countries are going to react?"

Another man rose to his feet, this one somewhat more aggressive than the last.

"But how can we possibly stop this movement?" he asked. "They don't break any laws. If people want to vote for them, how can we stop them?" I for one, will not be a part of anything that degrades our democratic principles."

The young Chairman turned sharply. "If you want to kill a snake, what do you do?" he shouted. "Do you go for its body? No you go for its bloody head, don't you? We must direct all our efforts to the leaders, to the inspiration behind this ridiculous movement. We all know who I mean; this man, who has the money and power to change the direction of the world, must be stopped. Someone this dangerous cannot be allowed to continue to inject his poisonous policies into the vulnerable population. If we value our society as we have known it for hundreds of years we must act now. We are not alone in these thoughts. All the governments of the Western world are with us, and even all the major religious leaders are behind us. This man threatens their beliefs and positions just as much as he does ours. They have all expressed a desire to join with us in our battle. Yes, gentlemen, I say battle, because that's what it is. This is a war between their insane beliefs and our civilisation."

As he sat slowly into his luxurious seat, he tossed his long blond hair to one side somewhat effeminately, reaching for the glass of mineral water and raising it to his lips. A wry, sinister smile slowly spreading across his previously intense face.

"I shall be taking control of the situation personally. My brief comes directly from the top. We must all give this matter utmost priority. I may be out of the country for a while; you can contact me through my P.A if you need me. Thank you gentlemen, I will be in touch soon to give you all your personal itinery."

With that, he rose quickly from his seat and strode over to the door, stopping along the way to whisper in his assistant's ear, and then quickly disappearing into the labyrinth of the corridors of secrecy.

# CHAPTER 23

_It was a black stormy night in Jindalee, a trendy riverside suburb of Brisbane, Queensland, Australia. The gale force wind was howling, bending the tall, wispy gum trees to almost breaking point. The leaves, torn from the branches, were swirling around in mini tornado-like twisters on the sodden ground. The droplets of rain glistened like golden beads, as they showered down past the one, single streetlight, which was illuminating the tall, wooden church hall.

A sleek, dark blue sedan pulled up suddenly, alongside the small side entrance, its door was flung open by someone in a hurry. A tall slender young woman eased her long slim legs out gracefully, placing her stiletto clad feet gingerly onto the soaked, slippery grass path as she jumped out of the car. Her long black coat flowed behind her as she hurried through the downpour and into the building. She stopped momentarily in the dark, dank vestibule to adjust her black silk headscarf so that it covered her long golden hair and her lean, tanned features, as if trying to hide her identity from prying eyes. As she opened the inner door and entered the hall, the people seated inside all rose and turned to greet her simultaneously. Their faces were illuminated by the flickering flames of the roaring fire situated at the far end of the gloomy room. Their heads swivelled to follow her, as she strode down the side aisle, turned to her left and mounted the three steps onto the small stage-like structure. She took her place at the central desk which was flanked on both sides by the other speakers. Everyone sat down after her, as if by an unspoken command, their faces staring in anticipation of their leader's eloquent teachings.

 "I am here tonight to address a problem, a problem the like of which we have never experienced before," she began, as she rose to her feet. "The problem of the movement, I am sure you are all aware of, and of which, I am sure, my fellow brethren here, have made you conversant with tonight. This damned political party that has transcended from politics to religion. Not since the Communist Party banned or tried to ban, all religions from the Iron Curtain countries during the Cold War, have we been under such a threat as we now find ourselves today. We all know what I am talking about. This so called party, that is sweeping through the world like an epidemic, has policies that undermine the very fabric of our society, and the total basis of our, and yes all other religious, beliefs. This movement must be stopped, and we are the ones whose duty it is to stop them. We will crush and obliterate them, as we would squash a mosquito.

"Look at what they say about religion. They say that all our evangelists were some sort of super beings; our Lord was what equates to being a conman, in some strange sort of supernatural contact with a deceased ancestor in heaven, who told him there is no God; that all mankind, whether good or evil, will eventually ascend to heaven. They say our Lord did not die for us on the cross, was not resurrected from the dead and was not the son of God. They say all our children must be taught these lies, taught to believe in their atheist ways, even to the extent of being taken from any parents who fail to carry out these ridiculous instructions. I ask you all here, is this the world in which we want to raise our children? Are these the teachings of a future leader of the world as he purports to be, or are these the teachings of a fanatical maniac?" Her voice rose to a crescendo.

"We've seen men like this before, we've seen what people like him can, and have done, to the world and we, as responsible members of society, have dealt with them in one way or another. We will deal with this man in the same way, but this time before he and his cronies wreak the havoc others like him have done previously. We will not shirk our responsibility, we will fight for what we believe in and we will win!" She slumped into her chair as if exhausted by her outburst.

All the audience jumped to their feet, cheering and applauding wildly, as if some kind of mass hysteria was gathering them up in one enormous moment of exaltation. They chanted hysterically in unison, "God will triumph, God is all powerful," over and over again.

The tall woman rose from her seat and walked to the side of the stage, her arms held aloft in a kind of triumphant salute, waving to the cheering crowd as she walked quickly down the aisle. All the others on the stage rose and followed her in procession, into a small room through a doorway which was hidden in the gloomy corner of the hall. As they entered, they all took their seats around a large, polished oak table situated in the centre of the room. The leader remained standing as all the others sat, in anticipation.

"You have all been allocated and notified of your tasks," she started in a commanding domineering tone. "Be diligent in your preparations and be thorough in you actions. Go back to your congregations and prepare your people, but, most importantly, make certain all of your influential contacts are made aware of the enormity of their responsibilities. I intend to take personal control of the situation. I promise you here

and now, that I will resolve this problem by whatever
methods needs to be employed. Make sure we are ready to
fill the vacuum that will be created when this evil movement
is destroyed, as destroyed it will be, have no doubt of that."

 With that parting comment still ringing in their ears, the
people seated saw their leader turn, bow to the crucifix on
the far wall, and disappear through the exit and into the
stormy night. They all looked at each other, a grim,
determined expression spread across their mesmerised
faces. These were dangerous people.

# CHAPTER 24

Jude closed the door behind him as he left the bathroom after his habitual early morning shower. As he dressed in the neat and tidy hotel room, he heard a sharp knock on the door.

"Come on, Jude," someone called. "Are you up and running yet, get a move on."

Jude strode over to the door and released the electric lock. The door flung open and in walked Jack, a broad beaming smile exposing his white glistening teeth.

"Well, today's the biggie, mate. If we pull this one off OK it'll be no stopping us eh." Jack shouted excitedly.

"Yeah, tell you what though, I'm bricking it," Jude replied. "This party conference has just got to go well. Today's got to be the day we start to change the world. It's payback time for all the folks who've suffered so much for so long. Come on mate, let's go get some breakfast. I feel like I'll need plenty of energy today."

Jack led the way out of the room. Jude following pausing as he went, to pick up his battered old wallet, his keys and his bulging briefcase, and pulling the door closed as he left. He heard the electronic lock click as the door slammed shut. Funny how he was always conscious of his security. He had been aware of his vulnerability for quite some time now; John had warned him often enough of the dangers facing him and his movement. They entered the lift and Jude watched the floor numbers light up as they went down, seven, six, five, four three, two, one and then ground. It jerked to a halt, the doors slid open and they walked slowly down the corridor and into the restaurant, making their way to the table with their number card on. Jude looked around, the place was almost empty save for a young couple about three tables away, they were laughing and giggling coyly, "Bet they're on honeymoon," Jack whispered. "They look happy anyway, don't they?"

Jude tipped the crunchy cornflakes into the plain white bowl in front of him. "I wish Mum and Dad were here now," he said, as he reached for the glass of ice cold milk.

"Yeah mate, they'd be real proud of you now," Jack answered. "Are you all ready, have you got your speech sorted?"

"It's all done and dusted, she'll be sweet, mate. The TV guys are all fixed up as well. I tell you Jack, today is going to make a lot of people sit up and take notice. After this afternoon the world will be a much different place. It's going to take time, I know, but this is the beginning of our vision, the first step on our journey. Geez mate, I've started already!"

"Yep, Jude, I think you're in the groove there, but let's have brekers first, eh," Jack joked.

Jude sipped the dregs of his coffee, wiped his lips with a serviette and rose from his chair.

"Let's get to it, then," he said in a self-confident, determined fashion.

They both strolled out of the restaurant taking the lift down to the basement floor where the car park was. As they turned the corner, they saw the car sitting elegantly in its bay. "That's a beautiful car Jude; those Poms can sure make a decent motor, eh?" Jack said. He flicked the key fob and the indicators blinked a couple of times. "Ready mate?" he said as he opened the door and slid into the plush leather driver's seat.

"Ready as I'll ever be," Jude answered. "I think I'll ride in the back if you don't mind. I just want to mull over a few things as we drive."

The limo glided out of the dark, damp, underground car park and into the glistening sunshine of a warm summer's day. Jack blinked as his eyes adjusted to the sudden glare, reaching into the glove box and donning his shades. Within minutes they were on the freeway. The car sped along effortlessly at eighty. "I know we're doing eighty, mate but it seems like thirty in this motor, don't it?" Jack said, as he swerved around a semi-trailer cruising in the centre lane. He looked in his mirror and saw Jude studying his papers intently. "Sorry mate didn't mean to disturb you, better not put on the old rock and roll tapes today, eh?" Jude didn't answer. He never even heard Jack, so engrossed in his notes was he, that he was oblivious to almost everything.

 SYDNEY 25 MILES the sign stated as Jack glanced up. "Won't be long now," he thought, "about another twenty five minutes and we should be there."

 "It's getting a bit muggy in here, Jude," Jack said, "Do you want me to put the air con on for a bit?"

 "Anything you like, Jack, I'm easy," Jude answered, "By the way; you know the route to the hall, don't you? Remember we're not going the normal way. We've been advised by the police to take the back route, it's quicker that way."

 "No worries mate, I've got the route down here. The map they sent us is stuck up here on the dash," Jack said. "Here's the sign now, next exit and we're off the freeway. Seems a bit daft to me though, it looks twice as far on the map as the normal way, still I suppose they know best."

Jack eased the car into the inside lane, ready for the next turn off and took the side road. It was a narrow, dusty track, not at all what Jack expected. They travelled down the road a few miles. "Do you think we're on the right road, Jude?" Jack quizzed.

"Yeah, carry on a bit; I'm sure it'll be OK," Jude said, more concerned with his speach than he was with the route.

"This truck's coming up a bit close," Jack shouted as a large, black Volvo truck appeared as if from nowhere and closed up to the rear of the car. "Is this guy asleep or what? Bloody hell, what's he playing at?"

Jude turned around quickly to see the radiator grill of the truck looming up in the rear window, about three feet away and closing fast. He could see the flies and mossies squashed on the scratched and dented bonnet, it was that close.

Within seconds, before anyone could do anything, they were spinning in a cloud of thick, choking red dust. Jude felt himself hurtling through the air. He didn't have time to ready himself for whatever might be about to happen. The last thing he saw was his papers flying past his eyes in a swirling blur, then, all of a sudden, complete darkness.

The black Volvo truck screeched to a halt about a hundred yards down the road, its tyres billowing thick blue smoke from the heat of the rubber. The driver, a slim tall man, smartly dressed in denim shirt and trousers, jumped down from the cab and hurried back to the car, looking around anxiously as he ran to the driver's door. He grimaced as he yanked open the twisted metal that was once the door. Jack was lying across the steering wheel; the horn was blasting, held down by the weight of Jack's lifeless torso. The truck driver reached forward and eased Jack slowly back into the seat. The horn fell silent, as he ripped the blood soaked route map from the dash, slipping it into the hip pocket of his dusty jeans. This was a quiet lonely stretch of road, but as he looked around he noticed a car in the distance, a tiny cloud of dust on the horizon. Quickly he ran to his truck, climbed into the cab and fired up the engine.

He swung the massive unit around and sped down the dusty road back towards the freeway. In an instant he was gone, and all that remained was the carnage he had caused. Jack was slumped back in the driver's seat, blood covering what was once a handsome face. Jude was lying in the red dusty road, where he had landed after being catapulted out of the rear door that was torn off in the impact. No birds sang, the air was still. It was total silence.

Jude opened his eyes. A blurred face slowly came into focus. 'Mm, she's pretty,' he thought to himself. 'Wouldn't crawl over her to get to most of the girls I've been out with.' A pained smile spread across his face. 'Can't be too badly injured if I have these thoughts,' he said to himself.

"Hello Mr Brown, you're back with us then," the young girl said.

"Where am I?" Jude stuttered.

"It's OK, you're in hospital. You had us worried for a while there," the young nurse said. "I'll get the doctor."

"No wait, how's Jack?" Jude shouted.

"I'll have to get the doctor," she insisted.

After a few minutes a young, prim doctor appeared.

"Hello Mr Brown," he said, "How are you feeling?"

"Bugger that, how's Jack?" Jude shouted.

"Take it easy, Mr Brown, you'll be fine in a few days. You were a very lucky man, just a few cuts and bruises and a bit of concussion."

"Listen mate, I won't ask again, how's Jack?"

"I'm sorry, we did everything we could," the doctor answered almost apologetically.

"You mean he's…?" Jude couldn't finish the sentence. Jack had been his best friend since day one. If it hadn't been for Jack he knew he wouldn't be here now.

"Oh God no, please tell me this isn't happening. How could this happen? Oh Jack, mate, I'm so sorry. If it wasn't for me, none of this would have happened. I can't go on like this.

There are so many evil bastards in this world. Oh John, help

me, please, if you can, please help?"

# CHAPTER 25

The rain was lashing against the window pane so hard that it woke me up. Have you ever woke suddenly to think, "Where the hell am I?" only to come to your senses a few seconds later? Well, this was one of those times. The only thing was a few seconds had passed, and I still didn't know where the hell I was. As I looked around, I saw I was in a neatly made bed with plain crisp white sheets, tucked in neatly and efficiently. The curtains were drawn all around the bed except behind me, where the window was. It was a tall, wide window with the top light open, in spite of the torrent outside, strange though, no rain was coming in. As my gaze wandered around, past the metal bars behind me supporting the fluffy striped pillow, I noticed a small tap jutting out of the wall. There was a small word written underneath. I strained my eyes to read what it said; I could just make it out, 'Danger Oxygen' it read.

It slowly became clear to me just where I was; I was in a hospital bed. 'Still,' I thought, 'by this time nothing could surprise me.' I heard footsteps approaching, faint at first, getting louder and louder. I expected a Nurse or Doctor to appear at any second but, as I peered through the gap in the curtain at the side of my head, I saw, to my amazement that the person who approached wasn't either of these; not a medical person at all. I rubbed my eyes to make certain. Yes, there he was, Jesus.

"Hello John," he shouted, as he pushed back the curtains to reveal the rest of the general ward. 'Strange that,' I thought to myself, as I looked around to see all the other beds sitting there, totally empty.

'What's happening?' I asked myself. I felt a tremendous sense of danger, my head hurt like mad. As I gathered my senses I began to realise what some of these feelings must mean.

"I think I'm experiencing something awful, I fear something dreadful has happened," I shouted. I had this deep unrest inside my head, "Jude is in terrible danger." As he had grown and matured, Jude had developed his own personality and thoughts. Even so, although we were not now as closely united in thought as we were when Jude was first born, Jude and I were still constantly aware of each others feelings.

"Why am I here in hospital? Help me, Jesus, I'm so confused."

"Calm down, John," he said.

"Think back. Go back to your time on earth, were you ever in hospital?" Jesus queried.

"Yes I was, when I was seven years old I was admitted to a children's Hospital with a mystery illness. The doctors were baffled at the time. It was only when my eyes turned yellow after a couple of weeks that they discovered I had jaundice," I replied.

"There you are then. You have sensed Jude has been involved in some terrible experience; you feel he may have been hospitalised and your only experience of being a patient in hospital was when you were yourself in hospital as a child. Do you know what's happened to Jude? Has he been in an accident, or do you think it may be something more sinister? I have told you many times of the dangers facing him during his life, haven't I? I fear he is in grave danger," Jesus said

rather abruptly.

 "Yes, you're right. I have the feeling this may not have been

an accident. Jude has told me recently he has had a few

misgivings about a certain events that have happened. He

has heard whispers of someone investigating his financial

dealings. You know Jesus; I've been having some horrible

thoughts lately. Do you think it could be possible for

someone here in the Perihelion to be assisting a person on

Earth to prevent Jude from fulfilling his goals in life? It

appears that there is someone always one step ahead?" I

asked.

 "John, as I've told you many times before, that sort of thing

would not be possible. There is no evil here; all pure energy is

without blemish. The only evil that exists in the entire

universe is unfortunately on our planet, Earth, and more

disconcertingly in our own people, the human race," he answered.

"In that case, could it be that some poor misguided person on Earth would be able to deceive a presence here in heaven into assisting them?" I queried.

"The only way that could possibly happen is if someone on Earth was able to disguise that part of his mind which contained the evil thoughts. To masquerade his mind as if it was normal. I don't mean he pretends to be some kind of saint. After all everyone on Earth still alive has some element of evil, unfortunately it's part of the human makeup. All I'm saying is he would have to appear as an average run-of-the-mill man or woman," he said.

"Do you mean he or she would have some kind of alter ego, like a schizophrenic for instance?" I asked rather tentatively.

"I suppose that is theoretically possible, John. I must admit I've never really thought about it before. I would think it highly unlikely though. It would take a remarkable coincidence for someone to have the ability to communicate with one of us here, be some kind of twin-minded person and be the one who wishes for some reason to persecute Jude in one way or another."

"What if I told you there may well be that person," I replied urgently. "What if I was to tell you I know of that person? I'm sorry Jesus, I must leave you, please excuse me. I must speak with Jude as soon as possible. I'll see you soon; I feel we will need your help before much longer."

# CHAPTER 26

_ A spine-chilling tingle ran down Jude's back every time he heard John's words echoing through his mind. The sentences John had spoken to him were reverberating to and fro inside his confused head. 'The person who is of most danger to you is possibly someone who is experiencing mental problems. Someone who suffers from a kind of split personality, probably schizophrenia or a similar ailment. That's the only way anyone with evil thoughts or designs could communicate with someone in heaven able to help them.' John had said to him. Jude was constantly turning it over in his head, over and over again. If this was the answer to whom Jude's assailant was, then there was a massive turmoil in his life. To his knowledge there was only one person in his life who could fit the bill. The only one who had experienced any mental problems of that kind was the one, most important person in

his life. His most treasured love, his precious Cherie.

 He and Cherie had been inseparable since that fateful day

their eyes had met through that fly screen door at her

Father's house. He loved her more than he had any other

thing in his short troubled life. He felt closer to her than to

anyone; yes even closer than he did to his mentor, John. He

and Cherie had lived and loved as one. Constantly,

passionately and completely. She was his life. The only thing

in Jude's mind was to hopefully, one day, marry her and

settle down to have kids and do the whole family thing. They

did everything together. Because of Cherie's phobia over

cars, Jude had even designed a special cycle for them, a sort

of tandem made for two, but with some slight modifications.

It was made of titanium for lightness, with the rear

handlebars brought forward in front of the forward seat so

that when Cherie was sitting behind him, her arms wrapped snugly around Jude's torso. Down each side of the bike were solid roll bars to protect them against any untoward events. It was the only way Jude could persuade her to travel on the roads. She flatly refused to even sit in any kind of motor vehicle. Strange though, she was fine on trains. She even managed the short flight from Brisbane to Sydney on a couple of occasions, but cars, no way.

On one occasion, when they were out on one of their many cycling expeditions to the beach, Jude almost plucked up the courage to ask her to marry him, but the moment somehow passed, and the time hadn't seemed right since. Anyway Jude was brought up with what many would consider to be old fashioned ideas nowadays; he wanted to ask her dad's permission first. Not many people would understand this quirky tradition in these liberated times, but Jude couldn't help the values instilled in him by his own father, in fact he was proud of them. Anyway, they both knew they would marry one day. It was a sort of unspoken inevitable conclusion to their love.

 In spite of all these feelings, Jude knew he must find out the truth; he must end these doubts in his mind, if not for himself then for John. After all, John didn't know Cherie as he did. He hadn't experienced her love, her generosity or her sincerity. He also knew he couldn't risk their future together by just simply asking her point blank about all these doubts planted in his mind by John. If he ruined their chance of happiness together and all these thoughts were proved to be without substance, he could never live with himself, it would destroy him and her. He felt he must rid himself once and for all of these terrible doubts, so that he could continue to love the one person in his life who meant everything; the one person who was his whole life. He decided what he had to

do. He must talk to Cherie's father, Joe, John's son. No, that

would not be the answer, oh who could help him, he

thought. Then it suddenly came to him. He couldn't believe

he hadn't thought of it before. The one who had convinced

Cherie of his sincerity all those months ago, Cherie's

grandmother, Ann, John's wife. It was strange how

everything in his life seemed to revolve in some way or

another around John. Jude reached eagerly for Cherie's

address book which was always left handy by the phone in

the apartment they shared, their love nest they called it. He

picked it up and flicked quickly through the pages. He knew

he had to ring the number immediately. If he didn't, then the

courage he had summoned would disappear, and he

wouldn't be able to go through with it. Jude was the kind of

person who acted instinctively and repented at leisure.

"Hello," the voice at the other end of the phone answered.

"Ann," Jude said, rather tentatively, trying to hide the quivering in his voice. "It's Jude, hope you are OK, Ann, I know this may seem a strange question, but could you tell me about Cherie's accident when she was a young girl, and the problems she had coping afterwards?"

"Why do you ask, Jude?" Ann said, rather startled, "Is Cherie ill? Oh I hope she isn't having a return to her mental problems again. I couldn't go through all that again."

"No, really, everything is fine," Jude answered, "We've just been having a few problems lately. Ann, can I be frank with you? Can I tell you something I've only ever told one person before, something only Cherie knows,  something about me and your John?"

"You mean about your physic contact with him? I'm sorry Jude, I know you made Cherie promise not to tell anyone but after that phone call when you two first met, I squeezed it out of her. Don't worry Jude, no-one else knows. I would never tell your secrets to anyone. You see Jude, Cherie inherited much from me. Many people say that traits often skip a generation don't they? Shortly after John died, I spoke to him in a dream. He told me how all the thoughts and premonitions I had had over the years we were together, were not the result of any mental depression and anxiety problems I had after losing almost half of my family. No, they were the normal reactions of a person who was more sensitive and receptive to the thoughts of others than most. I was always aware of these physic powers, I suppose you could call them. I don't mean being able to look into the future or tell fortunes or anything like that, I just experienced these dreams that allowed me to contact people who were no longer with us. I could do things I could never have done in consciousness. Cherie was the same, even before her accident. I always knew it wasn't just the loss of her mother that gave her these thoughts, they were always there. I tried to tell the doctors, but they didn't understand. What I'm trying to say Jude is that Cherie is just the same spirit as me. There isn't one once of harm in that girl's head. She is physically and mentally incapable of hurting anyone or anything. She is a beautiful caring honest girl, of that I'm certain."

"You needn't say any more, Ann," Jude said sincerely. "Everything's OK. It's me who has been having the problems not Cherie, but I'm sure that everything will be fine now I've spoken to you, honestly. Thanks for your help Ann, please don't tell Cherie about any of this, will you? I don't want her to worry. I love her deeply, you know."

"I know you do, Jude," Ann answered. "I hope you sort out your problems soon. If I can help in any way, please give me a ring. I know I'm a long way away but it's only a phone call you know. Bye for now."

"Bye Ann, and thanks once again." Jude replaced the receiver slowly and deliberately, a fixed stare on his troubled face. What Ann had said helped ease his worries a little. If only John hadn't said what he had, still, he was sure about Cherie now, wasn't he?

# CHAPTER 27

_Jude was startled by the intercom barking out its message.

He had been somewhat lazily languishing in his favourite

black leather office chair, staring out through large picture

window overlooking Moreton Bay, the natural marina of

Brisbane harbour. Not really looking at anything in particular,

rather just looking at all and seeing nothing. His thoughts had

been lost over what had been happening during the last few

weeks. Jack, his dearest and oldest friend was gone. Cherie,

his beautiful, loving partner was now the subject of suspicion

in his innermost fears. How could all this be happening to

him? All he ever wanted to do was to use his special gifts to

the benefit of his fellow man and help his people to achieve

their destiny. 'Am I such a bad person,' he asked himself,

'That I need to be punished like this?'

"Mr Brown," the squeaky voice at the other end of the line said. "There's someone to see you, a Detective Inspector Brady from the Interstate Police. Are you free to see him?"

"The Police, yeah OK send him in," Jude answered. 'Could this be something to do with the accident?' Jude asked himself, 'Maybe some of my questions will be answered at last,' Jude said to himself.

The tall slim young man walked briskly through the door into Jude's office.

"Mr Brown, let me introduce myself, Detective Inspector Brady, Interstate Police," he said somewhat arrogantly as he waved his warrant card ID in Jude's general direction. "I've been assigned to the case concerning your accident. I've been looking at your statement and wondered if you could clear a few things up for me?"

"Sure, I'll try," Jude said, motioning to the vacant seat opposite his. "Fire away."

The tall detective sat easily onto the chair, adjusting his jacket as if not wanting to crease it as he settled. He was a neat smart young man, not at all like the traditional policeman you would expect to see on any TV cop show. Rather trendy really, in his snappy, pale grey suite and black, patent leather fashion shoes. Jude couldn't help but notice the expensive Burberry socks as he crossed his legs, almost inviting anyone to see them. He was a well-presented man, long but modern styled hair topped his somewhat feminine handsome face. His piercing blue eyes darted around the room inquisitively. Settling comfortably into the supple leather seat he appeared to be completely at ease in the plush surroundings.

"Well Mr Brown, I noticed in your statement you said the route that you and your driver took on the day of the accident was on police advice, but I've checked with all the relevant people and I can't find any mention from anyone about the Police Service offering you any advice regarding the route you should take on that or any other day. Do you still have any correspondence that may throw some light on this?"

"No," Jude answered, "I seem to remember Jack, the driver, stuck it onto the dash of the car before we set off. Wasn't it still there in the wreckage?"

"No Jude, I may call you Jude can't I? Nothing was found either in the car or in the immediate vicinity of the accident. There was little or no wind that day either, I checked with the weather people, so I don't think it could have been blown away. You see, Jude, if there was no instruction about your route from the police then there's a good chance that letter was sent by the person who planned the assault on you; if it was a planned assault that is."

"But I saw the letter, I remember it distinctly. It was printed on official police stationary. I remember seeing the letterhead." Jude said rather abruptly.

"Please don't get me wrong Jude; I don't doubt your word. What I'm saying is that it was probably a forgery. I suppose anyone could have copied the letterhead from an original, after all it wouldn't be difficult," Brady suggested.

A sinister thought flashed through Jude's mind. He remembered Cherie telling him one of her Dad's businesses was a printing company; she used to help him with the paperwork, her being a bit of a whiz kid on the computer. Could she have somehow obtained the stationary from there? Cherie also used to do most of Jude's computer work. She had tried to teach him the basics once, but he was useless. He may me advanced in a physic sense, but anything to do with IT, and he was hopeless.

'Why am I having these thoughts?' Jude asked himself. 'How can I doubt her, when I love her so much?'

"Can you think of anyone who may wish to cause you harm?" Brady asked.

"Well, I suppose in my profession, there may be a few people who aren't too happy with the way things are, but I can't think of anyone in particular. Well no-one who would go as far as threatening my life, anyway." Jude replied.

"Jude, I can't offer you protection twenty four seven, you know that don't you. Have you ever thought of employing a security service, a bodyguard for instance?" Brady asked.

"No, definitely not," Jude answered emphatically. "How can I teach peace, and campaign against violence, while employing someone who earns his living by using his expertise to hurt people? It would be somewhat hypocritical don't you think."

"Maybe, but if that accident was a premeditated attempt on your life, you could be in serious danger. I know it may not be for me to say, and believe me I mean this in the best possible way, but have you ever thought of taking a bit of a back seat on the political front for a while, until things calm down a bit. It would give us more time to carry out our investigations, while giving you a bit more time to consider your future plans."

"No!" Jude shouted. "I have no time to spare. I don't want to sound as if I'm preaching Inspector, but I will not, nor cannot give up on my people. I will not relent in my goal. It is my destiny, I have no choice."

"Ok Jude," Brady said, as he rose from his seat rather suddenly, as if slightly annoyed be Jude's outburst, "Well I'll probably be in touch later, thanks for your time." With that parting shot, he turned and jauntily headed towards the door. Turning as he left, he said, "Take care, Jude, there are some dangerous people out there and it's usually someone who you would least expect, that turns out to be the most threat. Be safe."

Jude sat back in his chair. He was a troubled man, and he felt very alone for the first time in his short life. Even his closest kindred spirit, John, seemed very distant right now. What could he do next? Which way shall he turn? If only he was sure.

<u>CHAPTER28</u>

"Hello John!" someone shouted abruptly. The sudden greeting made me jump in surprise. I looked over my shoulder in anticipation; I don't know why I didn't recognise him immediately, after all, I had heard his welcoming, friendly voice many, many times by now; the deep Arabic tone of my dearest friend, Jesus.

"Hello, I answered, as I swivelled around to face him. I noticed something peculiar as I did so. This was a new experience for me since I had arrived here in the Perihelion. I was inside a building I didn't recognise. To the best of my knowledge, I had never been here before, and up to now, I had always been the one who chose were I was, or whom I saw, albeit sometimes inadvertently. As I looked around the large, dark, hall or room, I thought how much it reminded me of the old cinema that I used to frequent as a child. The only difference was the lack of the heavy brocade curtains around the stage, and the fact there were no flying, winged horses painted on the two side walls. Those paintings were a mystery to me for many years, until I realised what the name of the cinema really meant. It was called The Hippodrome and I must have been about eleven or twelve before I realised that it was the Greek word for the course where horse and chariot races took place. "Where are we, Jesus?" I asked inquisitively. "Everywhere I've been to up to now, has been a place I remember. I don't understand, I can't recall ever having been here before."

"No, John, you've never been here before, this is my invitation to you. You are seeing what my guest and I see, our thoughts are influencing yours."

"Your guest?" I replied somewhat surprised, "Who is it? I don't understand, where am I?"

Jesus turned and beckoned to someone who had remained concealed in the shadows. An elderly looking man emerged and approached us, his head slightly bowed as if he was ashamed or embarrassed over something. He was a pretty ordinary looking person, the kind of man you would see every day on your way to work. Plain average clothes, black shoes, short neat brown hair, in fact very nondescript. 'Do I see this man like this because I don't know who he is?' I thought to myself. 'I suppose it makes sense doesn't it?' "Hello," I said, rather not knowing what to say to be honest. "I don't seem to recollect meeting you before."

"Good evening John, I may call you John, may I?" the stranger said in a rather faltering voice. "Yes, you're correct, we have never met before, but I have known of you for quite a while. Let me explain. I came here to the Perihelion a short while ago, and I, as you maybe, was very confused and struggling to come to terms with what had happened to me. I reached out for help and fortunately Jesus heard my pleas and came to my aid. During our conversations, I told him of something I did whilst on Earth, something of which I am not proud, something of which I am very ashamed. I know now that what I did was very wrong. But hindsight is a wonderful thing isn't it? If only I could have found the truth about all this here, it could have been so much different."

"What did you do?" I asked, "that you are so worried over. You know when you arrive here; you don't come with any baggage. You have a clean slate here, everyone is equal."

"Well John, let me explain. I belonged to a religious movement. Our followers were very sincere, sometimes to the point of being almost fanatical. I now know we were so misguided. It was here, in this very hall, that I and some of my fellow members met, to plan our most important and urgent agendas. We all believed passionately in Christ and Christianity. We were taught to believe anyone who tried to attack or discredit our religion was to be treated as the enemy, the foe to be fought in the battle for man's spiritual purity. The last meeting I attended was to plan an attack on the movement called The Universal People's Party and its leaders."

"Hang on a minute; this is about Jude, isn't it?" I shouted.

"Let me finish, John, this is of great importance. You see from what Jesus has told me, there may be no time to lose. As I said before, the movement I belonged to was very passionate in its beliefs. Anyone who endangered our religious movement had to be stopped, stopped at any cost, in any way possible. Just before I died, I attended a meeting here in Jindalee, in this very hall."

"Jindalee, I remember that place. I nearly bought a house there when I lived in Australia; It's a suburb of Brisbane isn't it? I'm glad I didn't though. The whole place was sixty feet under water when the cyclone struck in the seventies," I added.

"I remember that John, it was an awful time wasn't it? But to get back to what I was saying." He continued, "As I said before, I was at a meeting here that was convened to confront the problem of the political party I mentioned before. Our leader came to address us and to brief us on our individual duties. She told us the name of the man we were to target. You were right in your assumption, John; it was indeed Jude, Jude Brown. When I confessed all this to Jesus, I had no idea you and Jude had this special connection. He told me about what was happening, and suggested I come to see you, and of course, I was only too willing to help. I simply can't believe I was involved in something that could be so catastrophic to man. How can I have been so stupid?"

"Don't blame yourself; there was no way of you knowing what was happening. After all, there are thousands of people like you on Earth aren't there? Brainwashed into believing what someone else has decided they want you to think is the truth. If only there was a way of telling everyone on Earth the real truth, the truth that we here all know." I said, "Anyway, tell me about this leader of yours. At least I may be able to warn Jude. Oh no, I've just realised, it was your lot who caused Jude's accident wasn't it?"

"I honestly don't know about that, John, but I wouldn't be at all surprised. Unfortunately, I died before any of the final details were revealed to me, but I can tell you they are certainly capable of such deeds. I'm afraid we don't know the names of any of our leaders, it's a security thing, and they all probably had false names anyway. None of us knew her name to the best of my knowledge," he replied.

"Her, you said her! Your leader was a woman then. What did she look like?" Doubts rose once more inside John's mind, the nagging doubts that kept coming back to haunt him.

"I never saw her clearly; our meetings were generally held at night, in dimly lit places, just as we are here. She always partly concealed her face with a dark veil but I know she had long blonde hair. Mind you, I suppose she could have been wearing a wig or a hairpiece, it would make sense wouldn't it? She looked an attractive woman though, quite young I think, she had the movement of a younger woman, do you know what I mean?" He moved his hands waving in a swirling motion as if to enhance his description. "That's about all I can tell you I'm afraid, John. I'm sorry I can't help you any more."

"No really, you've been brilliant, thank you very much." I said gratefully. "Jesus, I must leave, I don't wish to appear rude but I must contact Jude. I'm sure you understand, there isn't a moment to lose."

"No, John, you must not go just yet. There is someone else you must speak to." Jesus shouted, pointing to another dark mysterious corner of the room.

A tall lean figure lurched out from the shadows.

"G'day John, mate, I'm Ned Frazer," he said in a broad Queensland drawl.

He was a middle aged man, about forty or so I would say, dressed in a blue cotton shirt, open at the neck, dark brown cord trousers tied with a piece of string just below the knee, heavily scuffed brown leather boots and an enormous khaki bush hat perched on the back of his head. I was struck by his eyes, a piercing ice blue.

I knew immediately who he was. I remembered Bahlee telling me of the attack and murder of the settler called Frazer, all those years ago in the troubled early years of the colonisation of the Australian continent. I had never met this man before but this was how I imagined him to look; a sort of Ned Kelly person, whom I had seen in a film sometime in the distant past.

"I'm here to help you, if I can," he said in a deep growl. "Jesus has told me of your predicament, and I thought I may be able to shed some light on the matter, if you catch my drift."

I turned to Jesus and gave him a broad smile. "You've been busy, haven't you?" I joked.

"You know how I was killed by an aborigine, Bahlee, he was called wasn't he? One of your ancestors I believe. Well, mate, those were dark days," he said, "We were all pretty ignorant of the plight of the abos back then. We believed what we were told by the government men. They told us the darkies were a threat to us whites, that they were somehow subhuman. An uncivilised lot who would kill us and rape our women as soon as look at us. We were told that to kill them was somehow the right thing to do and we followed there advice to the letter. I am dreadfully ashamed of what I and the others did to them. I don't blame them for what they did in retaliation, but I have learned since I've been here, that many of my descendents were not so forgiving while they were on Earth. When they've arrived here they have told me about their lives being built on hate and retribution. I must say though, that I am surprised it has lasted this long. I thought by now the passing of time would have diluted the hatred many felt, but I fear I have been wrong. Time has not healed the wounds of some of my family, even today."

"Do you know the names of these people?" I asked.

"No, mate, unfortunately I don't," he replied, "but if you were to trace my family tree, or something, I think you may be able to come up with so some kind of clue. Maybe a name or place, perhaps. Sorry I can't be of more help, but if you need me again, please give us a call, mate."

"Thanks a lot, mate," I said to him, "I'll get in touch with Jude right now and fill him in." I would have liked to have talked with him a little longer but I think he really wanted to get away. He appeared to be deeply troubled by his past. No sooner had he finished speaking, than he turned and hurried, head bowed, back into the shadows. I turned to Jesus and said.

"I think that man is a very troubled spirit. I thought everyone here was forgiven their sins Jesus."

"Yes John," he replied. "We can forgive him but can he forgive himself?"

# CHAPTER 29

"I can't believe you asked my mum that!" came the cry from a very angry, and extremely emotional, Cherie.

"How could you, Jude. How could you possibly suspect me of wanting to do you any kind of harm, after all we've been through together?"

"I don't suspect you, Cherie," Jude pleaded. "Honestly I don't. I have been under so much stress lately I don't know what I'm thinking. Please, let's just forget about all this, love."

"Forget about it, you aren't serious are you? The only thing I want to forget right now is you. I'm sorry Jude, how can I ever trust you again? How can we be a couple, when it's

obvious what you have been thinking of me all the time?"
Just leave me alone. I can't even bear to look at you right
now, I'm leaving," she screamed as she ran out of the room,
grabbing her bag as she sped through the door, slamming it
behind her.

Jude stood there motionless. He knew he had taken a
massive gamble telling her about his call to her Gran, but he
couldn't run the risk of her hearing it from someone else. He
couldn't bear the thought of concealing his feelings any
longer. He would rather risk losing her than face the prospect
of living a lie.

After a couple of days, although it had felt more like a
couple of months to him, Jude plucked up the courage to pick
up the phone and ring Cherie. He desperately wanted to see
her, he hadn't realised how much she meant to him, but he
now knew he must arrange a meeting, even if she rejected

him he had to see her. He had been going to some of their favourite places where they used to hang out together, restaurants, pubs, cafes. Anywhere he thought he may bump into her, but she wasn't there. It was as if someone was determined to keep them apart, he thought, but he knew that wasn't the case. She just wasn't interested in him anymore, he convinced himself. He dialled the number and waited anxiously as the phone rang and rang unanswered. He was just about to put the phone down when a voice answered. "Hello," she said. Just the sound of her voice made Jude's heart miss a beat.

"Hi, it's Jude, remember me?" he said.' What a stupid thing to say,' Jude thought. In all the time he hadn't seen her, he had been rehearsing in his mind what he was going to say at this moment, and then he goes and says something so stupid. 'What a pillock,' he said to himself.

"Oh it's you," Cherie answered. "What do you want? I thought you preferred to speak to my mum rather than me."

"Please Cherie, can we talk, I've missed you ever so much. I love you, you know I do. I'm not taking no for an answer, if you won't come here I'm coming to find you." Jude pleaded.

"Ok, I've got to come round to pick up a few things anyway, I was hoping you wouldn't be there, but I suppose it doesn't make any difference really," Cherie said in a quivering voice, "I'll come round this afternoon."

Cherie arrived later that very same day. She had been waiting impatiently to rush round to the apartment but had deliberately stalled until the afternoon so as not to appear too eager; she didn't want Jude to think she had forgiven him for his mistrust in her. As she walked down the corridor to the door of the flat her legs were turning to jelly. What if

Jude rejected her? What if it was all over? She was almost unable to contain her feelings.

As she turned the lock and entered the room, Jude was standing in front of the window. He turned suddenly and their eyes met simultaneously for the first time in two days. They both knew at that precise moment that this was right; they knew they could never be separated again.

"I love you more than anything in this world," Jude said in an emotional outburst, "please forgive me? "he added, as she ran into his arms, sobbing.

They made love there and then, on the sumptuous, black leather sofa, as if they were making love for the first time, uncontrollably, passionately and tenderly. No-one or thing would ever separate them again.

The next day they were both awake early. Neither had really slept that night. Jude was first to rise, and he made her favourite breakfast, orange juice, French toast and a massive mug of steaming hot tea. As they lounged, partly dressed, on the settee, Jude turned to her and said, "Cherie, you're a bit of a whiz kid on the computer, aren't you? Will you help me with something? You know what I'm like on those things don't you, I'm useless."

"Yes, of course I will, love," she answered. "What are you up to now, another business venture, I suppose?"

"No, it's not actually. You know how someone has it in for us, well I've had an idea how I may be able to find out who it is. I want you to help me to trace a family tree. You see, from what John has told me and having thought about it, I've realised that this person must be someone with an almighty grudge against me. John told me about meeting a couple of spirits, for want of a better name. I know it may sound strange, but one of them told him about a woman who is the leader of a religious group who are out to stop our party at all costs. The other was someone murdered by one of our Aboriginal ancestors, you remember Bahlee don't you?"

"Yes Jude, I remember him, how could we ever forget after what we have inherited. OK, let's give it a go, we can't lose anything can we? Actually I've heard of a website that does that sort of thing, Genes Together, I think it's called, I'll get the lap top out, and we can do it now if you want, if you can control yourself for that long, stud," she joked. "I'll just have a quick shower first."

Cherie emerged from the shower after what seemed like an eternity to Jude, 'What do women do in there that takes so long?' Jude thought to himself. She walked over to computer desk, brushing past Jude; he reached out and grabbed the pink dressing gown hanging loosely from her shoulders.

"No you don't, we have work to do," she shouted as she tossed her long black wet hair sideways, showering him with water. She hurriedly sat in front of the computer, pressing the start button as she lowered herself into the leather office chair. Within minutes it was ready and she selected the search engine site.

"Here we are, Genes Together, just as I thought. Right, where shall we start?"

"Put in the name Ned Frazer. He was the one killed by Bahlee. That's what started this empire of ours, I suppose. See what comes up," Jude said.

"I'll have to subscribe first, just give me a minute" she said as she took her credit card from her bag.

Jude walked over to the large picture window at the far side of the room. He looked up into the cloudless blue sky, saying to himself, 'John could this be the beginning of the end?'

"Right Jude, that's all done," Cherie shouted. "Here we go!" She entered the name.

"It's come up with a few choices, what date did he die?"

"I think it was about eighteen fifty seven," Jude answered.

"OK, this looks interesting," she said, as she pressed the enter key. After a few seconds the screen flashed up part of the family tree.

She scrolled down the page; Jude peering over her shoulder, gently stroking her damp hair.

"Stop!" Jude exclaimed, "Scroll back again."

A name leapt out at them from the screen, a name they both recognised instantly. Well two names actually, a boy and a girl, brother and sister, both direct descendants of Ned Frazer.

"Look at that," Jude exclaimed, "Twins,"

"Yes, and according to this the girl died at birth," Cherie added.

"She must be his contact in heaven," Jude said. "That's why he could fool her into believing his mind was pure. She would have wanted more than anything to believe his mind was pure. She would have trusted him without question."

"What do you mean?" Cherie asked.

"Well, John said someone on Earth is getting help from someone in heaven, and the only way that could happen is if the one down here could fool the one in heaven into believing they were completely honest, some kind of split personality thing." Jude retorted.

"I see, that explains why you had doubts about me," she said, in a rather more understanding tone. "Why didn't you tell me all this before?"

"I didn't want to worry you, love," Jude said, as he nuzzled his nose on her cheek, "Please forgive me. John was right though; it is someone with a grudge, and what a grudge! Come on love, we can't stay here, pack a case. I know where we'll be safe; we'll jump on the boat and head up north. I have a lot of friends up there; no-one will ever find us. Once you're safe, I'll get in touch with someone and sort this out, once and for all."

They each hurriedly threw some clothes into a case,

strapped them onto the trusty tandem, and within minutes

were on their way to the Marina.

"I'll tell John what's happening, maybe he can help," Jude

said, as he pushed hard on the pedals. "Don't worry love,

we'll be OK, I'm sure."

# CHAPTER 30

_No-one saw the slow, rhythmical line of bubbles oozing gently to the surface of the calm blue water. Everyone in the marina was busying themselves with their daily chores, or lying on the decks of their luxury cruisers, soaking up the warm sunshine. Someone or something was swimming swiftly, submerged and hidden by the deep water, towards the white sandy beach of the secluded inlet around the headland. As the trail of bubbles neared the shore, the surface of the water broke in gentle waves onto the pale golden sand and a figure slowly emerged from the surf, clad in a black, rubber skin-diving suit, the sunlight glistening on the bright yellow air tank strapped to his or her back. Someone was in a hurry to reach the dark limo parked, partly concealed by the thick lush vegetation and trees lining the narrow dirt track leading to the beach. As the figure approached the car, he tore the clinging rubber helmet from his head, exposing the shock of blonde hair and handsome, somewhat feminine features of his face. It was a face very familiar to Jude and Cherie; it was the face of Detective Inspector Brady! He ran over to the car boot and jerked it open suddenly, as if in a hurry to get away. Peeling off the tight, clinging diving suite, he reached into the car and took out a neatly folded pair of ladies blue trousers and a dark grey blouse. Slipping these on, he then did an amazing thing. He pulled from the boot a long blonde hairpiece and positioned it carefully on his head, stooping to peer into the passenger side mirror, and adjust the wig, so that it sat perfectly as he wanted it, partially concealing his face with the long fringe. He pulled his car keys out of the pocket of the blue trousers, slipped into the driver's seat and fired the engine into life. The limo sped down the narrow lane in a cloud of dust. It was a very powerful car, a distinctive car, in fact the same car that had pulled up outside the church hall on that stormy night in Jindallee, the night of the meeting of the religious group so intent on Jude's demise.

The engine of his cruiser spluttered and groaned. "Blast it," Jude muttered, "Of all the times to pack up the damned engine's decided to do it now." He opened the hatch that led to the engine compartment. "Won't be a sec, love," Jude said as he squeezed past Cherie and disappeared down the dark damp opening. The blinding white light that exploded in his face was too sudden for him to respond, or to realise what was happening. The next thing he heard was a dull thud and he felt the cold water splash around his head and engulf his body. When he opened his eyes, all he could see were the bubbles swirling around his head, as if he was in a whirlpool of immense power. He felt the sensation of hurtling deeper

and deeper, the darkness enveloped his senses, his lungs

bursting, he couldn't stop himself gulping mouthful after

mouthful of salty water, as he gasped for breath. After a few

seconds, as he regained a little of his composure, he realised

he must act quickly or succumb. He thrashed his heavy arms

and legs about frantically, trying desperately to swim

towards where he thought the surface may be, but it was

hopeless. He could see a faint glimmer of light as he stared

upwards, but it was so far away. As he struggled vainly,

tiredness began to overwhelm his limbs. His arms and legs

felt like lead, almost too heavy to lift, he was losing his fight

for survival. As he slowly drifted upwards his eyes focused on

a face smiling down at him gently. It was his Mother as a

young girl; He recognised her beautiful features from photos

his father had shown him many years ago. The only things he

had seen to tell him what she looked like. She appeared to be laughing and crying at the same time, she was perfect. Suddenly another face appeared before his eyes, it was his Father, smiling with the expression of any proud parent looking down on their precious child. Cherie was peering over his shoulder, laughing childishly, as only she could do.

Jude focused his senses. He realised he was seeing his life flash before him, just as he remembered someone once telling him happened when you are drowning. He made one desperate last effort to reach the surface. As he struggled manfully he could see he was getting closer every second, but he knew deep in his mind that he wasn't going to make it. He was beginning to resign himself to his fate. 'Maybe I'll find out soon if my beliefs are to become reality,' he said to himself. The darkness deepened until he couldn't tell if his eyes were open or closed. 'This must be the end, or could it be the beginning?' he chillingly thought to himself.

Suddenly, he felt warmth in the palm of his hand; someone's fingers were folded around his. The strong tight grip was hurting his wrist, as he felt himself being hauled unceremoniously upwards, faster and faster towards the ever increasing brightness above. The instant his mouth and nose broke the surface of the water, he gulped down mouthfuls of cool sweet air into his bursting lungs, then the darkness returned as suddenly as it had seemed to disappear as he slipped back into unconsciousness.

"Jude, Jude, are you back with us love?" a voice whispered faintly in his mind. Jude opened his eyes, slowly blinking in the brightness surrounding him. As he looked around, not knowing where he was, he saw he was in what appeared to be a hospital bed. The neatly folded covers reminded him of the last time he was convalescing after the car accident. Then he realised where he was, he recognised the familiar surroundings. It the ward he was in before; in fact, it was Jude's favourite nurse leaning over him smiling warmly.

"Didn't think we'd be seeing you back here so soon love," she said jokingly.

"Yeah, sorry to surprise you, Carol, didn't think I'd be back here so soon either," Jude replied. "To tell you the truth I still don't really know what's happened."  A horrified expression suddenly spread across his face as Jude began to remember the recent events.

"Oh my God, how's Cherie?" Jude shouted, "Is she alright? Please tell me, Carol, she isn't badly hurt is she?"

"I don't know Jude; I didn't see anyone admitted with you. I thought you were on your own when you came in. Look love, you appear to have a visitor, maybe he'll be able to tell you more."

 Jude turned his head towards the door of the ward. A tall middle aged man was approaching briskly. As he got nearer, Jude was able to focus his blurred vision on the stranger's face, he looked vaguely familiar. As he stopped at the side of the bed Jude said to him, "Are you a doctor? Do you know how Cherie is? She was in the same accident as me, is she ok?"

 "Cherie's fine Jude, don't worry, she wasn't hurt at all. She was thrown clear, don't worry lad." The stranger said in a broad Pommie accent.

 "Have I met you before?" Jude asked, "Were you one of my Doctors the last time I was in here? How do you know what happened in the accident?"

"I know about the accident because I was there, Jude. You nearly ripped my fingers off when you grabbed my hand."

"It was you. You saved my life," Jude stuttered emotionally, "How can I ever thank you. Please excuse me for not remembering your name, Doctor."

"No Jude, I'm not a doctor," the stranger replied. "You probably recognise me from a photo you may have seen in Cherie's house, and you don't have to thank me for saving your life. I'm very sorry lad, I couldn't save you, I would have done anything to do so, but it was impossible."

"What do you mean?" Jude asked anxiously.

"I couldn't rescue you Jude. I would have if I could, you know that don't you? You see, lad, my name is John, John Lynch. It appears man has succeeded in destroying yet another chance to determine their future. Welcome to the

Perihelion, Jude, welcome to the future!"

The Doctor strode confidently and swiftly into the hospital ward, making a direct beeline for Cherie's bed which was situated at the far end of the long narrow room, separated from the main ward by a partition, the bottom of which was solid and the top half glass. Through it Cherie had been staring longingly in a vain hope that Jude would come. She knew there was no chance of that happening, Jude was gone, but she couldn't stop herself hoping. It just didn't seem real; she kept hoping she would wake and discover it was all a dream, a horrible nightmare, but she knew the nightmare had come true.

"Well Cherie, it looks like you'll be fine," the tall, dark, handsome Doctor said, in a reassuring tone. "All the tests are

OK, and I think you can go home tomorrow, all being well," he added, thumbing through the pages of the folder he was cradling in his hand.

"I'm very sorry to hear about your partner, Mr Brown. Have you someone to stay with when you go home? You shouldn't be on your own at a time like this, you know."

"Thanks Doctor, but my Dad will stay with me for a while; I'll be fine, really I will." Cherie replied, a tear slowly welling up in her reddened eye.

"That's good, I know this must be a really hard time for you right now, but don't worry, I'm sure you will feel better soon. When the baby arrives you'll probably be too busy to think of anything else, won't you?" he said.

"Baby, did you say baby? You mean I'm pregnant doctor? I'm having a baby, we're having a baby, can you hear me

Jude, we're having a baby!" she screamed. "Can you hear me, can you hear me?"

My eyes blinked open, I could hear someone shouting me, 'I bet I'm late again,' I thought, as I reached down to pick up my trousers from their regular nightly resting place, on the floor at the side of the bed. As I looked around the dimly lit room, I realised where I was. Yes I was back in the bedroom at my Mother and Father's house where I lived when I was at Grammar School. Not yet another of those flashbacks again. I made my way down the steep, bare wooden stairs and opened the door rather tentatively. 'Yes it's another hallucination,' I said to myself, as I peered through the dense fluffy clouds, 'I'm in heaven. Or am I? Oh no, are these clouds or is it steam? Oh, it's not bloody washday again is it?'